INTERVIEW TACTICS™

How to Survive the Media Without Getting Clobbered!

"The Insider's Guide To Giving A Killer Interview!"

by Gayl Murphy,
Hollywood Correspondent

www.InterviewTactics.com

INTERVIEW TACTICS is available in bulk quantity discounts for bulk purchases. For more information about bulk purchasing, please eMail the author at: Books.@InterviewTactics.com.

Or, you may write to the author at: GAYL MURPHY PRODUCTIONS, 1300 N. Cahuenga Boulevard, Suite 118, Hollywood, California 90038.

For information on how individual consumers can place orders, please visit the web site: www.InterviewTactics.com

INTERVIEW TACTICS™

How to Survive the Media Without Getting Clobbered!

"The Insider's Guide To Giving A Killer Interview!"

by Gayl Murphy,
Hollywood Correspondent

www.InterviewTactics.com

Copyright Notice

"You Gotta Tell It To Sell It!" ™

- Gayl Murphy (Murphy's Law!)

TABLE OF CONTENTS

Acknowledgments & Dedication

A Personal Message From The Author

Introduction

PART ONE:
IT'S A MEDIA JUNGLE
OUT THERE! *1*

❏ Getting Media Savvy! 6
❏ Lights ... Camera ... Action! 7
❏ "You Gotta Tell It To Sell It!" 7

PART TWO:
GIVING THAT KILLER INTERVIEW! *11*

❏ Where Am I? Testing, Testing (1 ... 2 ... 3 ...) *13*
❏ What Is A Killer Interview And How Do I Give One? *13*
❏ What Does A Reporter REALLY Want? *14*
❏ How Do I Give A Reporter What They Need? *15*
❏ But, What If A Reporter Doesn't Give Me What *I*
    Want? *19*
❏ How DO I Prepare To Talk To The Press? *20*
❏ This Is A Test Of The Emergency Broadcast System
    This Is Only A Test! (Yeah Right!) *21*
❏ Helpful Hints For Finding Your Story *21*
❏ Be SPECIFIC! Give DETAILS! Write PARAGRAPHS! *22*
❏ A Special "Heads Up!" For "Showbiz" Media Virgins! *23*

PART THREE:
THE TEST!

.... 25

❏ What's The Best Way To Get My Message Across? 28
❏ Now That I'm Prepared ... What's Next?- 29
❏ What *Is* The Point And How Do I Get There? 30
❏ Am I Allowed To Ask Questions? 32
❏ What If The Press Asks Me About Something I Don't
   Want To Talk About? 33
❏ What If The Reporter Continues? 35
❏ What If The Journalist Starts Badgering
   Me For Answers? What Do I Do Then? 36

PART FOUR:
LET'S GET TECHNICAL!

.... 39

❏ What's All This About Soundbites? 41
❏ Great Soundbites Throughout History! 42
❏ Dressing For An Interview! 44
❏ What Language Is Your Body Speaking? And What Is
   It Saying About You? 46
❏ Is It OK To Be Funny? 47
❏ Is There Really Such A Thing As "Off The Record"? 48
❏ Not All Interviews Are The Same! 49
❏ TV Interviews 49

PART FIVE:
THIS IS WHERE IT GETS GOOD!
"HURRAY FOR HOLLYWOOD!"

.... 53

❏ Questions You Get To Ask During The Set Up
   Of Your TV Interview! 55
❏ Smile For The Camera! 56
❏ What The Heck *Is* All This Stuff? 57

❏ Remotes Aren't About Control, Or "What Do You Mean
 I Have To Sit In A Room By Myself?" 59
❏ Press Junkets And Roundtables 60
❏ Roundtable Interviews 61
❏ Radio Interviews 62
❏ Anyone Can "Wrap" 63
❏ Getting Ready For Radio 65
❏ Radio Remotes And Radio Tours 65
❏ Print ... The *Windy* Medium 67
❏ Think Color, Think Detail And Be Specific! 69
❏ Press Conferences And The Red Carpet 69
❏ The "Media Darling" And How To Become One! 72

ALMOST THERE 75

THAT'S A WRAP! 81

THE HOLLYWOOD "TALK OF FAME" 89

INTERVIEW TACTICS WORKBOOK!

   WORKBOOK: 🖎 **PART ONE!** 111

   WORKBOOK: 🖎 **PART TWO!** 127

   WORKBOOK: 🖎 **PART THREE!** 131

   WORKBOOK: 🖎 **PART FOUR!** 135

Meet The Author

Interview Tactics Coaching

Interview Tactics Seminars

Gayl Murphy's Web Site

*Interview Tactics Partners
& Associate Resources*

Book Order Forms

ACKNOWLEDGMENTS
&
DEDICATION

INTERVIEW TACTICS is dedicated first and foremost to each and every person who's ever sat down in front of my microphone and had a chat with me. Thanks for giving me the opportunity to help you tell your story. You don't know how much you've changed my life in so many ways. Through your myriad of experiences, you showed me a slice of the limelight that I was able to learn from and use, and for that I will always be grateful.

I could not begin this book without first acknowledging the many media people, journalists, reporters and producers all over the world who have touched my life. Specifically, the L.A. Press Corps in all its configurations and those of us who cover entertainment news including lifestyle, films, television, music, literary, sports and popular culture.

My heartfelt thanks to all the jocks at KROQ Radio in Los Angeles, CA, in the late 1970s, at the birth of my broadcasting career. Most importantly, Stanley Sheff and The Young Marquis who gave me my break, but not forgetting Frasier Smith, Rodney Binginheimer and the late Tree who produced my first voice-over demo.

KWST Radio in Los Angeles, CA, where I really learned to play with the big kids: in the mornings with Phil Hendrie and Raechel Donahue, JJ Jackson, Dusty Street, Steve Downes, China Smith, Radio Rich, David Perry and Ted Ferguson. Was it really that long ago?

KLOS Radio in Los Angeles, CA, where I learned to *"keep on rockin' in the free world"* while working along side and learning from Michael Benner, the boy genius, and Larry Jacobs who gave me my first interview assignment. Steve Downes (again), Uncle Joe Benson, Shana, Jim Ladd (the Lonesome LA Cowboy), Rita Wilde, Geno Mitchellini, Bob Coburn, Chuck Moshontz,

Al (Dog) Ramirez, Bill Sommers, Jeff Pollack, Tommy Hadges and the late B. Mitchell Reed.

To Bill Ratner, the first to ask me the all important question: "Do you really think someone's gonna pay you to *talk* to people?" Love you Ratty!

At ABC News in New York, I am grateful for having learned from and having been inspired by giants like Steve Jones and Merrille Cox.

At the BBC News bureau in L.A., a big thanks to Andy Hollins and Peter Bowes.

To the BBC in London including Robert Nesmith and the folks at *Liquid News*.

To all the members of The Broadcast Film Critics Association, of which I am proud to be a member.

To all the national reporters, writers, producers, on-air talent and correspondents (of whom there are too many to mention) who gather at *The Four Seasons* and other L.A. hotels to talk to the stars. A big "Thank You" to those who currently sit at those tables with me now!

To all the companies - network, record, studio, management - and publicists with whom I've worked over the years.

I'd also like to thank the "Original L.A. Radio Gang" who were there when I first arrived on the scene and who showed me only kindness and were amazingly inclusive: Mike Reynolds, Mary Lyon, Jane Platt, Howard Benjamin, Suzanne Whatley, Shep Morgan, Denise Cox, Joey Berlin and Laura Gross.

To all my friends and family, especially Shirley, Sig, Ruth and Desta for almost "getting" what I do for a living.

To Kathleen Flynn, Chiara DiGeronimo and Barbara Tennant for being "the goils." To John Henry Kurtz, Jon Deckard, Bill McGowen, Randy Burton, Luaine Lee and Charles Kipps, just because.

The *Learning Annex* for the opportunity to talk to people one-on-one and to all my cyber pals at Pho.

To Bart Smith, a.k.a. TheMarketingMan.com, who helped me maneuver my way through the online, self-publishing jungle and the art of *"book title naming."* *Interview Tactics*, the title and domain name, was brainstormed and birthed by TheMarketingMan.com. Titles are everything I'm learning, and you came through for me 125%. I would also like to thank Bart for helping to craft and design the entire book layout including the front and back cover artwork. And, how can I forget the web sites: www.GaylMurphy.com and www.InterviewTactics.com. Do you ever sleep, Bart? You are … *"BBBBart to the Bone!"*

To John Lahmeyer, whose invaluable editorial skills brought my manuscript to life, thank you so much. John is a talented editor and an associate of Bart Smith, TheMarketingMan.com.

To Larry Terenzi, for the 11th hour reading. You'll always be *Mr. Showbiz* to me!

And to the lovely and talented actress who enabled me to finish my book on a positive note.

To all of you, I am sincerely grateful.

Gayl Murphy

A PERSONAL MESSAGE FROM THE AUTHOR

Interview Tactics! It's MORE Than Just Surviving The Media Today!

... And thank goodness for that! I know the title of this book *says* "How To Survive the *Media*," but the truth is INTERVIEW TACTICS is much bigger than just the *Media*. Having an arsenal of "interview tactics" is about surviving and flourishing in *any* situation that requires you to step up, respond to questions, tell your story, peak your listeners' interest and wrap in up in 30 seconds or less!

As you may have noticed, our culture is becoming more "media-ized" everyday, and that puts a whole lot of pressure on our ability to just "say it" ... as in talking succinctly about what it is we "do." I'm convinced all this attention grabbing is reeking havoc on our morphing attention spans ... all because we're so stretched for time.

Experts say we are bombarded with so much information and advertising - about 3,000 ads a day, 21,000 per week, or a whopping 1.1 million per year - that some of us have actually started talking to each other in soundbites over coffee and bagels. And these "soundbite people" are starting to expect the same from us. And guess what? Soon the rest of the world will be demanding a soundbite or two from you. Will you be ready?

So, how can a regular guy or gal with a story to tell, or something to sell, compete in this "information free-for-all" and not get clobbered? It's been my experience, that *if you can't tell it, you can't sell it* ... regardless of what you're trying to say. And, that includes selling your self, your skills, your company, your car, your product or service, or just sweet-talking your honey into being your Valentine.

It's true that *Interview Tactics* is tailored for making the most out of meeting the press, but the "power tools" I have revealed inside *Interview Tactics* are also a sure-fire way to give anyone the one-two punch they need to get their story and message out there in the terrain of our soundbite culture.

Interview Tactics will provide you with all the expertise and insight you'll ever need to go one-on-one in *any* situation where you're put on-the-spot; have to step up to a microphone, podium, telephone; pitch a meeting at a big wig lunch or in an executive boardroom and tell your story.

And that's the truth, the whole truth and nothing but the truth. So, buckle-up my friends and get ready to *tell it to sell it*!

Gayl Murphy

INTRODUCTION

Interview Tactics was written for anyone who has ever wanted to step up to the microphone and tell their story to the world! And there are plenty of you out there.

As a veteran Hollywood Correspondent for some of the most prestigious news services in the world, I've had the good fortune to interview, have a little lunch with, and generally "hang" with some of the most famous "movers and shakers" on the planet. And, I've conducted thousands of interviews for radio, TV and print with some of the biggest celebrities, including award-winning actors, actresses, pop stars, musicians, writers, directors, producers, artists, authors and business people ... and that's not the half of it.

I've also spent a good deal of time interviewing new and upcoming "media stars" as well, including the next generation of celebrities, inventors, lifestyle gurus, teachers, fitness experts, business tycoons, chefs, decorators, designers, how-to authors, do-it-yourselfers, and what I call, the *experts next-door*.

After spending almost two decades in the company of these media stars, both the "newbies" and the "oldbies," and genuinely being impressed with their stories and accomplishments, it was always a surprise to me when the rest of the world didn't have a clue who they were. If I found their efforts compelling and intriguing and I wanted to tell their story, why wasn't the rest of the press following suit? Why weren't they singing their praises too? Somebody was being left behind here and I was sure it wasn't me.

Then it dawned on me, the reason these guys and gals were missing the media-boat was because they "couldn't tell it to sell it." They didn't know how to talk to the press, they were clueless about how to package their own story and they didn't know how to connect their dots in a media-friendly way. Worst of all, they had no clue as to what the press wanted from them!

Surely, I thought, there must be some kind of "media rehab" somewhere! A training program perhaps, or a book. Maybe a video that caters directly to *media virgins*, Corporate Kings and Rising Stars everywhere? Some kind of straight-ahead, no holds barred, how-to manual that lays out *"Murphy's Law"* ... **"You gotta tell it to sell it!"**

Well, there wasn't. So I took it upon myself to investigate and find out why. I went on a mission and I worked like a fiend. I scoured the web, went to seminars, visited bookstores and interviewed many of my media pals ... "How does one survive the media without getting clobbered?" I asked. I poked. I prodded. And much to my shock and amazement, no one could tell me definitively HOW TO SURVIVE THE MEDIA WITHOUT GETTING CLOBBERED!

A lot of my colleagues told me about media training classes and workshops where they show you which end of the camera is up and how to sit and stand and where to look - which, believe me, is valuable to know - but I found no Media Survival Holy Grail ... no Interview Bible ... no Interview Tactics ... not a single shred about *how to tell it to sell it and survive the media* at the same time ... and, no insider's guide to giving a killer interview either! But what I did discover instead was a niche ... for myself, and a darned good idea for a book!

I talk a lot in *"Interview Tactics: How To Survive The Media Without Getting Clobbered. The Insider's Guide To Giving A Killer Interview* about the *expert next-door* and then I realized ... I am one!

I've interviewed thousands upon thousands of the world's "one-percenters" in my broadcast and news reporting career, and the time has come to spill the beans on the media and let the world know what the heck they really want when they sit down with you to do an interview. And in doing so, I discovered that I could also show-and-tell the next generation of superstars how to go one-on-one with reporters like me and not get clobbered. You see, by the time you get to me and my kind, I've already done three interviews before your interview, I have two more after your interview and I can only tell one story per day. So, what is it you're going to tell me that's going to push your interview to the top spot?

So just when I was feeling comfortable about the task at hand, my friend, Mylene Dane, a non-media colleague, shook me to my senses after hearing about *Interview Tactics*. Mylene loved the idea for this book so much that she made me promise I would say something to Interview Virgins of the Corporate Kind, and what they're up against when they're being interviewed.

"Why should I address people being interviewed for corporate jobs?" I said, "I think there are enough books around for them already, don't you?" "Not enough," she snapped back. "In these harsh economic times, anything that we can get our hands on that will help us *tell it to sell it* in business, is something we need and want to know about! You think *Interview Tactics* is just for people struggling to survive the media, but it's not. Because when you're interviewing for a job in some bigwig's corporate office, you might as well be the lead story on *60 Minutes* because that's what it feels like! The amount of scrutiny nowadays is unbearable. You better know how to *deliver* in a way that's going to grab these honchos right out of the box too! *Interview Tactics* not only teaches people how to tell their own story, it also shows them how to find it, feel it and wrap it up into a variety of different packages that are friendly, informative and to-the-point!"

And she's right. We do live in a soundbite culture ... on and off the airwaves. So to all you Interview Virgins of the Corporate-Kind who aspire "to tell it to sell it" ... *Interview Tactics* is also for you, so come on down!

Gayl Murphy

PART ONE:

IT'S A MEDIA JUNGLE OUT THERE!

PART ONE:
IT'S A MEDIA JUNGLE OUT THERE!

"I didn't think about celebrity when I first started out as an actor. You know, you don't think about the effects of when you give an interview - what that's gonna mean ... I didn't think about that. But I guess as you grow up - and I've been doing it - and I realize that it's OK to say how I feel about things. I'm enjoying it and I feel comfortable and relaxed (being interviewed). I feel comfortable with you right now." ★ Tom Cruise

It's a media jungle out there. Vast, uncharted and sometimes really scary. An endless thicket of technology and "stuff" with its own language, its own customs and in some cases its own life forms ... so be very careful where you step ... and tread lightly my friend, 'cuz you could get clobbered! But don't take my word for it, just take a good look around this densely populated landscape and check it out for yourself. What *is* all this stuff? And all this "in-demand, on-demand, gotta have it" technology? What's that about? And who are all these people anyway?

In the last twenty years or so, our collective media taste buds salivated to such a degree they developed the most awesome case of the "media munchies," ever! Munchies, so raging that we feed, need and breathe every conceivable kind of media and information there is. TV, radio, newspapers, books, magazines, videos, video conferencing, CD's, DVD's, eBooks, CD-ROMS and the Internet ... and that's just the nonfat stuff!

Getting the picture yet? In my opinion, the bottom line is: we don't care what we munch on or who delivers it, just as long as we get it when we want it ... and we want it NOW! Cable, wireless, satellite, broadband, AM, FM, UHF, DSL, dial-up, streaming, fax, palm pilots, pagers and the "good ole" telephone. All these technologies - expensive, intricate and hi-tech delivery systems - just to get up-close-and-personal.

But, up-close and personal with who and what? From this insider's perspective, it's information and expertise. Sound advice and good old fashioned "how-to." We want to hear from authorities, experts and celebrities; we want the lowdown and we want it now baby! So, how cool is that?

Well, it's *really* cool if you happen to be one of those insider experts or specialists with something to sell, tell or share. Or, if you're this week's hot rising star in your field, you've got the gift of gab and you can work the media and talk to the press. If so, then let 'er rip. Imagine all that media attention, access, and ability to have people see and hear you in a media-friendly way.

Our raging appetites for this kind of personal, one-on-one, insider info from well-informed and articulate experts is mind-boggling!

My technology friends insist that it's just a matter of time before our ability to see and hear from these rising new media stars on-demand will soon be as close as our cell phones and palm pilots. We'll be able to instantly plug into these "info-shamans" by dialing them up from the convenience of our kitchen counters, treadmills, seaside loungers and wristwatches. At the touch of button, we'll instantly access interviews, advice and even media presentations from just about every kind of celebrity and expert you can imagine. And by the time you read this, it's probably already happening!

Just think of it, getting the lowdown right from the horse's mouth anytime, anyplace, anywhere. Award-winning and world-famous scientists, thinkers, successful business people,

www.GaylMurphy.com

singers, dancers, internationally famous chefs, statue-holding actors, writers, sports stars, sweating exercise mavens, bankers, advertising gurus, new-age nutritionists, lifestyle coaches, teachers, race car drivers, and the list goes on and on and on.

And in case you haven't noticed yet, most of these media babies aren't that much different than you and I, in that we all started out the same way: with some really great knowledge and information to share. The difference between you and them is they're media savvy. They know how the media works, what the media wants and how to give it to them.

"Charlie Rose has this uncanny ability to allow anyone that's on to be the 'smarter self' they are."
★ *John Travolta*

These savvy little darlings have perfected their media craft into a high art and allowed it to become second a nature to them. They can waltz right up to a press tent, talk into a microphone, look into a camera and "deliver," without compromising for one second who they are.

Think Jack Nicholson, Whoopie Goldberg, Ted Turner, Rudi Gulianni, Colin Powell, Deepak Chopra and even Richard Simmons. And what an incredibly valuable skill this craft is. Just don't kid yourself, it takes a lot of personal insight and lots and lots of practice to go from being a *media virgin* to a media star.

So what about you? And where are you in this big, bad media jungle anyway? You're a soon-to-be-superstar in your chosen field and I know you've got what it takes to give the world the "next greatest thing," but what will you do the first time (or the next time) a reporter walks up to you and says, "Got a minute?" Hopefully, you'll say, "Sure!" But, I'm also hoping that you're asking yourself two very important questions: "Do I have what it takes to tell my own story?" and, "Is it possible for me to survive the media without getting clobbered?"

GETTING MEDIA SAVVY

"In two hours you really can't explain who you are and someone can't really grasp who you are. They can only sort of get a taste." ★ *Cameron Diaz*

If you're like the majority of *media virgins* and *experts next-door*, you have no interview tactics. And, like them, you're also not aware of what's involved with packaging your story. More importantly, you don't know how to graduate from being a *media virgin* to a *media darling*. *(You're a media virgin when you don't know the difference between your PhD and your EPK!*)*

◆ **How do you get media savvy?**

◆ **How do you get media trained?**

◆ **How do you talk to the press and give a killer interview?**

◆ **How do you tell it to sell it?**

Now don't start beating yourself up because you've done interviews before and they turned out to rank among the most horrifying episodes of your tender life - even though going into them you were convinced you were "the media messiah."

Believe me, getting media savvy is about acquiring a specialized skill and it requires an insider to guide you through it. What to do; how to do it; how to speak, stand and look; what to think about; what not to think about and how to tell it to sell it. All these things must be learned.

And, this is exactly what *Interview Tactics - How To Meet The Press Without Getting Clobbered: The Insider's Guide to Giving a Killer Interview* is all about and why it was written. Fortunately for you, you've come to the right place. You have arrived! So get ready because here it comes!

EPK: Electronic Press Kit

www.GaylMurphy.com

Lights ... Camera ... Action!

"(The interviews) with which I've been most impressed with were the one's that have actually been truest to what I remember what I had said."
★ *Kelsey Grammer*

As a veteran entertainment reporter/correspondent/journalist and member of the international press corps, I estimate I've interviewed over 10,000 actors, actresses, singers, entertainers, directors, writers, producers, experts, artists and all form of celebrity in my radio, TV and print career!

So, if there were any secret facts or yet undiscovered truths I could tell you about being interviewed they would have to be deemed ... MURPHY'S LAW ... which is the very foundation and cornerstone of Interview Tactics and the *only* way to survive the media!

MURPHY'S LAW
"You gotta tell it to sell it!"

Being interviewed isn't as easy as it looks!
... And, not everyone's good at it!

It pains me to tell you how many times I've sat down to interview some high-profile somebody and they were so unprepared to tell their story that the entire interview was unusable. And the reason the interview was unusable was because **they didn't tell me anything I could use**. They weren't able to tell the story ... their story. (And, no I'm not going to tell you who they were so fuggedaboutit!)

I'm not saying that these nice people didn't have valuable things to say, share or sell. It's just that when it came right down to their ability to talk about themselves, their product or their specific skill or talent in media-friendly way, they didn't have a clue what they were *supposed* to say, do, or how to respond to questions.

The reason is … **they just didn't know how to be interviewed!** They had no insight or idea about the interview process or how it works. They didn't have any first-hand knowledge of what *the job of a reporter and the media is, and what the reporter and the media wanted from them.* Poor little *media virgins.* They were out there flopping around like tuna without a net. And, what was I supposed to do, my job *and theirs*? I don't think so.

Numerous times I've witnessed colleagues toss an interview entirely because the person they were talking to just didn't know how to answer questions in a media-friendly, usable way. (I'm still not telling you who it was.) These poor little *media virgins* were clueless about their *role* in the interview process - and why not? I mean, where do you go to learn how to talk about yourself unabashedly at great length, in colorful terms and in increments of twenty seconds or less? How much more unnatural and unspontaneous can you get?

We're living in a time when even your scruffy, preteen, skateboarding, next-door neighbor is being interviewed for TV, radio and print. And you've got something valuable to sell and promote too, so you've gotta ask yourself, ***"Will I be ready when my big break comes?"***

These days, the celebrity brand is not longer exclusive to handsome hard bodies and sculpted leading ladies, although I'd be lying if I didn't say that having a great face and gorgeous body doesn't help. Everybody wants their "15 Minutes" - or at least look like they've having it. And, with the explosion in the media jungle - especially reality TV - you don't have to be in show business to be a star!

Experts of all kinds - entrepreneurs, web tycoons, authors, artists, actors, actresses, CEOs, inventors, teachers, doctors, professors, chefs, animal trainers, scientists, appraisers, lawyers, athletes, designers and the like - are all being booked for interviews. And these aren't dull industry publications and hokey cable TV shows either. It's *everything* from network news to late night talk shows to CNN. It's HGTV, ESPN. The Cooking Channel, Bloomberg, PBS, FOX News, MSNBC, MTV, VH1, The Golf Channel, E!, Discovery Channel, C-SPAN, The History Channel, *Antiques Roadshow*. For crying out loud, it's the World Wide Web!

Being media-savvy and knowing your way around the press these days is no longer exclusive to "rich and famous" celebrities in Hollywood. Consider my pal Bill McGowan who recently wrote and produced a high-end promotional sales video for a client of his. With the right lighting, sound, editing and effects, he put together a promotional marketing package for this manufacturer that looked like the trailer of Dreamworks' most recent blockbuster. It was fabulous, informative, cutting edge and totally glam.

In my humble opinion, the most significant thing Bill did was take the company's camera shy CEO and coach him in the ways of the Hollywood media machine for three grueling days prior to the shoot. Then Bill plopped him down in front of the camera and started shooting. To everyone's amazement, this guy was so comfortable in the spotlight that he started chatting to the camera about himself and his company like nobody's business.

His transformation was mind-boggling. Watching this guy rattle on so, you'd swear he was some big shot movie producer on *Entertainment Tonight* who just snagged a three-picture deal at Universal! What I'm saying is **he knew what he was supposed to do and he delivered!**

In recent years, television networks, both here and abroad have made a killing in the ratings with reality shows, ongoing sagas of brave souls withstanding hostile environments. But let's be truthful here for just a second, when those people finally managed to get off those stupid islands and back into the real world ... did any of them really survive the hostile landscape of media jungle? Maybe one or two out of how many? And they were on TV every week!

For some movie stars, celebrity chefs, sports figures, real estate tycoons, new age gurus, *media darlings* and the like, chitchatting endlessly about themselves at the Four Seasons Beverly Hills over spicy tuna rolls comes quite naturally, like a gift from the media Gods. But for most *media virgins* and *experts next-door*, it's not that way at all. They have to work *really hard* at it and in some cases - no matter how they try - they'll never really get comfortable tooting their own horns.

Like any learned skill, having an arsenal of *"interview tactics"* for giving killer interviews takes practice and training. But no stress here, because in this fun-filled, action packed, media "tell-all" slash guide, we'll cover all the ins and outs and ups and downs of how to give a killer interview and how to handle people like me and my friends in the process.

> *"With the advent of satellite television and magazines and all kinds of publications ... everybody knows everything. There is no, "Oh in New York and in the big cities, they're so much more sophisticated then they are (anywhere else). No, everybody knows everything."*
> ★ *Joel Silver, Director*

PART TWO:

GIVING THAT
KILLER INTERVIEW!

www.InterviewTactics.com

PART TWO:
Giving That Killer Interview!

Where am I?
Testing, Testing ...
(1 ... 2 ... 3 ...)

"It's fun to talk about yourself and have everybody stare like they're really interested."
★ *Steve Martin*

What Is A Killer Interview And How Do I Give One?

Giving a killer interview is all about knowing how to talk about yourself without reservation.

Giving a killer interview comes from what John Travolta calls your "smarter self." It's that same authentic place inside your brain that got you where you are today, baby!

Giving a killer interview is about knowing how to comfortably explain about yourself *with* and *to* another person.

Giving a killer interview is about knowing how to go one-on-one with a journalist or a group of journalists to tell and sell yourself, your business and/or your project, so the world can know all about you, what you've accomplished and what your next step is.

Giving a killer interview and being media savvy is a specific, learned skill. It's also an extremely valuable asset in the world of business ... and I mean ANY BUSINESS.

If you can navigate through the media jungle, you stand a chance at acquiring some of the most influential and important allies there are in the world, and that's the press.

So, if you're planning on meeting with a reporter anytime soon and you can't tell your own story, then ask yourself, "Who in the world will?"

Now don't get all sad and sappy on me now because you're clueless. All is not lost ... there is a way in ... there is a secret ... and the secret is ...

MURPHY'S LAW

If you know what a reporter is there for ... if you know what that reporter wants ... then, you should be able to give it to them.

What *Does* a Reporter Really Want?

"My particular path is to not give too much away. I try and intrigue the audience." ★ Jeff Bridges

First and foremost, the top priority of a good reporter or journalist is to stay employed. The best way for them to accomplish this is by turning in great stories - stories that are compelling, honest and brimming with information and insight.

The basic mechanics of a reporter's job is pretty consistent from story to story (i.e., Who? What? Where? When? Why? and How?) although it does vary from assignment to another.

On the entertainment, lifestyle and sometimes the business beat, what a reporter wants is to capture the essence - good and bad - of a person/artist/ project/company and explain that essence to their readers, viewers or listeners.

www.GaylMurphy.com

For better or worse, the journalist who will be sitting across from you is your gatekeeper. What that reporter wants is to interpret you to the rest of the world. But, they'll never tell you that. Keep in mind that a good reporter can only report what you provide them, either verbally or with your body language.

Sometimes the task of interpreting you depends on the reporter and their outlet. For example, the reporter for *The Star* has a very different agenda than the reporter for *Good Housekeeping*.

For some media outlets, the job of the reporter is to make you look good and to give the public what they want to see and hear. For others, it's not. So with this in mind, your assignment *before* the interview is to find some commonality here. What I suggest is to do some homework and become informed. Is the reporter friend or foe?

Who is this person and what do they want from me? Mike Wallace or Howard Stern? National Public Radio or *National Enquirer*? Not everybody is going to love you and not everybody wants to be your friend, so be a Boy Scout and be prepared.

How Do I Give a Reporter What They Need?

"I try to be a good interview because I understand what it's like to have a crappy one." ★ **Carson Daly**

A good reporter wants an **inner-view** of you.

MURPHY'S LAW

A *killer interview* is one where the reporter asks you a question, you answer it and then you elaborate on the answer with detail and color, giving the interviewer a place to go next.

For example ... This is how you *don't* want to answer a question:

Q - *"What's your favorite car?"*

A - *"A Chevy."*

(Thanks so much for making me work this hard.)

Now look at a usable answer to the same question:

Q - *"What's your favorite car?"*

A - *"My favorite car? My favorite car is a 1957 Chevy Bel Air. Nose decked with four on the floor. My dad had one in the garage years ago when I was a kid and he and I completely restored it, we'd work together on weekends ... Blah, blah, blah."*

Now, think football for a second and visualize the reporter as the receiver. The usable answer just gave the reporter somewhere to go next. We just had a little team work action going on here. I, as the reporter, now know something about you. I know that you like cars, you're somewhat knowledgeable about them, you worked on them as a kid and, I also know you had a sweet relationship with your dad, even if it was the only thing you ever did together. This is all great stuff for my article for *Parents Magazine, Car and Driver* or *Men's Health Journal*. By fattening your answer with colorful and informative bits of information, what you've given me is a "jumping off" point - and you've also helped me create my next question.

This is also an example of how you ***don't*** want to answer a question:

Q -*"So tell me, what inspired you to invent your new line of Chinese take-away food?"*

A -*"Because I like Chinese food."*

(Can somebody please throw me a chopstick?)

A usable answer to that same question might be:

> Q -*"So tell me, what inspired you to invent your new line of Chinese take-away food?"*

> A -*"I invented 'Chinese Food in A Bag' because I've always loved Chinese food. Moreover, when my wife was pregnant and we moved back to Milwaukee, she was craving Chinese food all the time. Anyway, I had the hardest time finding good Kung Pao Shrimp at 2:00 A.M. ... blah, blah, blah."*

Thank you, now I have somewhere to go, especially if I'm writing for a Milwaukee newspaper, *Bon Appetite, Business Week* or we're on the air at *The Food Network.* Are you getting this yet?

My favorite "no-no" answer actually happened to me. It was a really heavy press day, and I had just done 12 interviews back-to-back. I was talking to this hot young *media virgin* about the new teen movie he was starring in and I asked him what his next project was, and this is what he had to say ...

> **"My next film is a really big movie and it stars a lot of really famous people." ★ Annonymous**

Some answer, huh? I didn't ask him what the movie was or who the "really famous" other people were, because I just didn't have the energy ... *he couldn't tell it and he didn't sell it!*

MURPHY'S LAW

Think Details! Think Color!
Have energy and take me *to that place!*

> **"Some people do understand you, some don't and sometimes it can be very superficial." ★ Sting**

And it's OK to practice on a friend - you can tell them I said so.

At this point, I'd like to say something very important about "one word" answers ... FORGET IT! DON'T DO IT! Especially, "Yes" or "No" .. even if both are true.

"One word" answers will stop your interview in its tracks!

I'd like you to make a list of at least three different ways to say these one word answers. Write them down and practice them so that you start using them in your daily life. Need help?

"You're so right."

"I can confirm that."

"It's definitely true."

"You betchya!"

"How did you know that?"

"I don't think that's the case."

"I wouldn't say that."

"By no means."

"Not at all."

"Absolutely not."

"Not true, nothing could be further from the truth."

"I have no plans ..."

Another sweet trick when being interviewed is, along with saying the name of your product, is to try to include the name of the person who's interviewing you ... assuming it's comfortable for you and you can pull it off without sounding like a suck-up. Go ahead and compliment them on their question too.

Using the "Chinese Food in a Bag" example, the trick might sound like this:

> Q -"So tell me, what inspired you to invent your new line of 'Chinese Food in a Bag'"

> A -"You know George, that's a great question. I invented 'Chinese Food in A Bag' because I have always loved Chinese food and when my wife and I moved back to Milwaukee she was pregnant and was craving Chinese food all the time. Anyway, I had the hardest time finding good Kung Pao Shrimp at 2:00 A.M. ... blah, blah, blah."

Clean and to the point - and people love it when you say their name. They also really like it when you acknowledge their intelligence. So go for it, what the hey ... play the game ... and win!

Did someone say, **"Ya gotta tell it to sell it!"?**

But, What If A Reporter Doesn't Give Me What *I* Want?

"(An enjoyable interview) depends on who you're talking to. It depends on the quality of the questions." ★ Kevin Spacey

In other words ... what if your interview is one of those unlucky interviews where the reporter hasn't done his or her homework and thinks you're someone else or has no idea who you are and what you've been up to - what then? Whatever do you do? First, don't lose your cool, just accept it and forgive them of their sins, and then get that slacker up to speed as fast as you possibly can.

My dear friend, Charles Kipps, tells a story about when he was on the publicity tour for his book "Out of Focus." Charles was doing interviews all over the country and he was getting pretty good at it too. So he pulls into this one particular TV station and while he's getting his microphone pinned on and a bit of powder on his nose, the host of the show leans over to him - while the director is counting down, "We're on in 10 seconds ... 9 ... 8 ... 7 ..." and says, "So tell me, what's your book about?" (Yikes!)

Most journalists should and will tell you right off the bat, "I was up late night on a breaking story and I wasn't able to look over your material. Can you fill me in on what you do or what your book, workshop, TV show is about?" And that's fair enough.

> *"You sit there and they know my biography. I don't know your first name. I don't know anything. Already there is an inherent unbalance."*
> ★ *Matthew McConaughey*

Every now and then, you'll get some *B.S.* artist and you're only choice is to rise above it. My advice is to take the reins without taking over. Be cool and polite and just deal with the business at hand. After all, we've all been in a situation sometime in our lives where we weren't the person someone thought we were. Mistaken identity, sort of like, "Don't I know you? Didn't we go to high school together?" So just straightened it out. There is no need to embarrass the person. Move on with the interview and do your best. *"Shine on you crazy diamond."*

How DO I Prepare To Talk To The Press?

> *"Generally I have a good time when I'm doing (interviews), but ultimately I'm not crazy about hearing my own voice."* ★ *Jim Carrey*

Ralph Waldo Emerson said, "You are what you think about all day long." And that is so true. It's also something to keep in mind while attempting to survive the media. If you want to give a killer interview, I urge you to take the time and think about your life and decide how you want the rest of the world to perceive you, your product, your company and your achievements.

www.GaylMurphy.com

This Is A Test of The Emergency Broadcast System ... This Is Only A Test! (Yeah Right!)

"You can never really get prepped for this. You hear stories where people have gone through media classes to prep themselves, but we got thrown into it." ★ Joey Fatone (*NSYNC)

We've now come to the "virtual" audience participation portion of our journey. How to talk to the media and how to find a story to tell ... YOUR STORY!

In order to do this (i.e., find *your story*), you're going to have to ask yourself some of the following questions. And, while you're asking, let yourself and your mind go. Don't censor yourself and don't stop thinking about your story. Later on, when we break open the *Interview Tactics Workbook* (at the back of the book), you'll really have the opportunity to fill in the blanks.

So, for the time being, just stay focused on the questions and your response to them. Although, if you do feel compelled to jot down some answers now, feel free. For that matter, if it's helpful for you to start the *Interview Tactics Workbook* now ... *go for it!* (See Page 111) Just be sure you only do PART ONE!

Helpful Hints For Finding Your Story

You know how athletes talk about being in the *zone* when they're playing? Sort of like those scenes in the movie *For Love of the Game*, when Kevin Costner, playing the pitcher, steps onto the mound and uses the voice inside his head to clear the system so he can shut out all the outside noise. The *zone* is that special place where all champions go in their heads, it's the place inside where it's just them and the ball and the game and where they want to go next.

Well, you've got a *personal zone* in your head too, and I want to go there and hang out for awhile with your product, invention, songs, investment guide, videos, expertise, formula, procedure, lifestyle advise, script or whatever.

www.InterviewTactics.com

And while you're in there answering these questions, I'd like you to think along the lines of ... "If I were at a party and meeting new people, what is it about my life/job/profession/ creation that would other people find interesting?"

I'd like you to get connected, familiar, close and intimate with those parts of yourself, your product and your personality.

Be SPECIFIC! Give DETAILS!
Write PARAGRAPHS!

Q - "What exactly is it that you're doing?"

Q - "In a perfect world, how would you like the world to know you?"

Q - "How would you like the world to know about you?"

Q - "When someone uses your product, service, reads your book, eats your cookies or hears your music, what message do you want telegraphed and what do you want them to know about you?"

Q - "What is so unique about you, your medical discovery, movie, project, product, company, or whatever? How are you different from those who came before you and/or your competition?"

Q - "What's the most interesting thing about it? Go there in your mind's eye and revisit that place. Be specific. Think color and detail."

Q - "Just how DID you get interested in what you're doing? Take a walk down memory lane and be specific."

Q - "Why would someone want to read or hear about you? Don't worry about being egocentric, this assignment is for your eyes only."

Q - "If someone were reading about you, what would you want them to know? Why? Be specific."

www.GaylMurphy.com

Q - "What is it (exactly) that you have done that is so extraordinary?"

Q - "Just how colorful, dangerous or emotional was the rocky road to success? Now's your chance to really sell it. And here's a clue, chose one thing and elaborate on it."

MURPHY'S LAW

If your life, product or service isn't interesting to you, how in the world is it going to be interesting to anyone else?

A Special "Heads Up!" For "Showbiz" Media Virgins!

Actors: You will be asked to describe your character, to share a story or two about what it was like shooting the movie when the cameras weren't rolling and how you got the part. So, make sure you ask yourself those questions.

Singers/Songwriters/Bands: You will be quized on your latest projects too. And, those questions, no doubt, will be about your latest single, CD and tour. So, get in there and find your story.

PART THREE:

THE TEST!

PART THREE:
The Test!

"People are complex. You just have to give what is essential for the interview." ★ Cameron Diaz

Now, if you chose to actually write down some of your answers or you used *Part One* of the *Interview Tactics Workbook*, then go over what you've just written and bullet-point each and every item of each and every answer. Then, highlight all those bite size pieces of your story and set them aside. Be ruthless, edit like crazy and be as specific as you possibly can. There should be lots and lots of information to work with now.

What this process is about is creating a shorter and more detailed overview of all the different facets of your personality, persona and product all in one body ... yours. These are what I call your *talking points.*

When the time comes that you actually start giving interviews, every reporter with whom you'll be talking will be looking for a different angle on your *talking points* and, in doing so, they'll be looking at you from a different angle. You need to know and be intimately aware of all of your *talking points* so you can call on them at a moment's notice.

You might do ten interviews in a row and not be asked once why you invented Chinese Food in a Bag, but for that all-important eleventh interview, why you did it might be ALL the reporter wants to talk about. So do your homework and again **think detail** and **think color**.

Remember, your invention of the world's snazziest, new toilet bowl might not be the most interesting, colorful or earth shattering product to the person sitting next to you, but there are millions of plumbers, building contractors and homeowners all over the world who will think, "You really rock!" And maybe, just maybe, Home and Garden TV and Bob Vila are dying to make you a star!

What's The Best Way To Get My Message Across?

"If my words are twisted in a way that's not true ... then, hey, it's life. It's more important that I know who I am." ★ Halle Berry

Carpe diem, baby! You're the *expert next-door*, so take every opportunity you can to put it out there, even though sometimes a journalist won't want to hear it. If you want that feature story to include a lot about you, your movie, your record, your business, your show, your invention, your web site, then you're going to have to bring it up. Keep in mind though, there's hard selling and there's over selling, so be careful. It's a fine line and you're gonna have to find it and feel it out for yourself.

Some good examples of self-promotion:

I call this technique "weaving." "Weaving" is when you *gently* weave the name of your product or project throughout the conversation.

> "When I first decided to make *Gone With The Wind* in 3D, I knew the story had been done before, but I also knew the idea of *Gone With The Wind* in 3D was something that would grab people's imaginations again."

> "People ask me all the time how I came up with the idea for *Bernfeld's Cookies*. It came from my mother Shirley Bernfeld, the originator of *Bernfeld's*. When I was a kid, she used to make *Mrs. B's Cookies* for all the kids' birthdays and what's really great is, if you

like *Bernfeld's Cookies*, you can order a dozen or so online at www.BernfeldsCookies.com."

Now That I'm Prepared ... What's Next?

"I would say to just be honest and to enjoy it and have fun with it and realize how incredibly fortunate we all are." ★ Drew Barrymore

OK, let's get started! Now that you're beginning to understand what it means to tell own your story, do you think you can "tell it to sell it"?

Sure you can, as long as you remember to do it honestly and in an open, informative and descriptive way. You're a storyteller and that's what you're doing, you're telling a story - only it's *your story*.

It's crucial to keep in mind: telling your story is a give and take process and that you're not conducting a lecture here. This isn't "monologue time" even if the person you're telling your story to doesn't seem to be responding to you within your own personal rhythm.

Try getting a vibe from the person, engage them non-verbally ... something as simple as eye contact. Remember, it's perfectly normal to have lulls in any story, so don't be afraid of the quiet. And, if you must say something, try ... "You know what I mean?" or, "Do you have any questions about this?" It's a good idea to practice pausing yourself too, especially if you know you tend to be long winded and get up on your soap box.

In telling your story there are three very important points to keep in mind: the beginning, the middle and the end. And it's vital that you're clear on which is which.

Moreover, you must know where all these junctures are at a moment's notice, so if you have to, you can go back to them and get to the point.

What *Is* The Point And How Do I Get There?

"There's a job to be done here, but there's only so much you can do in 15 minutes." ★ Ray Liotta

Your job is to set yourself apart from the rest and grab the interviewer's attention and sense of imagination. The best way to do this is to start at the beginning of your story. A good beginning happens right out of the starting gate with a definitive tag or pitch ... almost like an opening statement that pretty much sums up who you are and what the heck you're up to.

But what if you don't have a tag or a pitch, how do you get one? Go over your *talking points* and your notes and work with them as if you were assembling words for a Scrabble game or assembling those refrigerator magnets that make up phrases.

Ask yourself, "If I, or my special interest, company or skill were a book, what would my title be?" Think of a grabby sentence or phrase and then another one right behind it that explains or supports the first one in an informative way. If you had to package your *talking points* in two sentences or less, what would they sound like?

> "I invented *Chinese Food in A Bag* for Chung Pao Shrimp addicts everywhere. It's my version of Cantonese 'brown bagging' it."

> "As the *Money Doctor*, I've discovered that saving can be a waste of time if you don't know what you're saving for. In my video, *Money on Life Support. The Ten Steps to Keeping Your Money Alive*, I reveal the prescription for getting rich and staying rich."

> "I'm an 87-year-old Granny on a mission. I wrote my book, *Rollerblading for the Young at Heart*, to let people know you're never too old to be young."

www.GaylMurphy.com

I suggest making a trip to your local bookstore and check out some of the latest, hot titles in search of a grabby opening. You'll be amazed at the length of some of them and how much information is crammed into two sentences.

Check it out. This is a great exercise because it trains your mind to think and speak your *talking points*. It's also an opportunity for you to feel what 20 seconds feels like. If you can set the stage in 20 seconds, can you imagine what you can do in 20 minutes?

Please note that I'm not suggesting that you abandon your ability to converse or speak in complete thoughts and sentences. What I'm attempting to demonstrate is - *should you find yourself in a crunch-time situation with a reporter or interviewer, and you've only got moments to lay your story out - this is the best technique I know to make the best of a bad situation.*

It's also a great technique to use in an interview when you have to explain something technical or use some specific scientific terminology and you can see the interviewer's eyes start to roll back in their head as they pass out from boredom.

Try to keep it as simple as you can by breaking down that tech-talk (as much as you can) and converting it into a language another human being can understand. Imagine you're explaining what you do to an astute 14-year-old. What metaphors would you use? Which ones would you not?

These questions should also give you some insight into how much the reporter knows about what you're talking about, and it's also inclusive. You never want to talk down to a reporter or interviewer because they're there to learn about you from you.

> **"I know the gig, you know the gig, I don't want to make it like pulling teeth. That's just painful for everybody." ★ Cindy Crawford**

Am I Allowed To Ask Questions?

Absolutely! All the time and why not? Jump right in there and break that ice. Show that journalist what a great person you are and that you're interesting:

"How are you?"

"How about those Lakers?"

"What kind of interview is this?"

"Who is this interview for?"

"Where is the interview going?"

"Where can one read, see or hear it?"

"How much time is necessary?"

"What is the general purpose of this interview?"

"Do you have any additional questions?"

"Do you know what I mean?"

"Have you ever tried this?"

"Has this ever happened to you?"

You can even ask about a reporter's background, where they're from, where they went to school and if they've ever tasted your award winning barbecue sauce. Actually, they'll be pretty stoked that you showed that much personal interest ... and trust me, it will win you points.

There's something else to consider. A reporter/interviewer wants to have a good time too. And they also have an ego, so show that you're interested in them as well. It's OK to suck up a little too, just don't tell anyone I told you so.

www.GaylMurphy.com

A great example of someone who does this kind of, what I call "adorable sucking up" is actor Sean Hayes from the show *Will and Grace*. Hayes has a way of nuzzling up to an interviewer that is so endearing. That no matter who he's talking to, he'll say with a huge smile ...

"That's such a good question and I'm glad you asked it." It's really nice to be acknowledged for doing your homework even though he says that to every reporter.

Don't forget, while you were out last night till 3 in the morning, cocktailing and dancing the night away, that reporter sitting across from you was most likely scouring the web researching and checking you out. Don't condescend to him or her, and don't forget to make eye contact either.

Keep in mind that whoever is interviewing you is really doing you a huge favor by getting your name, product or company out there. They're giving you free publicity, publicity that you'd normally have to pay a lot of money for. Here's a little advice: it's always nice to show some respect.

"You try to get into a situation that's productive and positive and not adversarial." ★ Tim Robbins

What If The Press Asks Me About Something I Don't Want To Talk About?

"I say something in a certain way and it gets printed - even if you're writing exactly what I'm saying - sometimes things get misunderstood." ★ Lisa Kudrow

MURPHY'S LAW
Always Try To Be As Truthful And As Honest As You Can!

Nobody wants to be lied to. If you **have** to hedge a little, do it *carefully,* and honesty is a requirement. Better to be boring than to be caught in a lie. If you can't tell a reporter when the stock is going public or that the famous navy blue dress from The Gap really belonged to you, then you better tell them something that will make it OK.

Example of respectful hedging:

> *"I've heard the rumors too and to tell you the truth, for me ... I stay out of that part of the business. I go to work, I do my thing and I don't pay much attention to what the other scientists are saying around me. I stay out of it and do my own thing."*

> *"It would be inappropriate for me to comment. Plus, we both know it would be against the law for me to do it publicly."*

> *"If you wouldn't mind, I prefer not to talk about that, it's a bit too personal. Is that OK with you?"*

> *"I'm really not comfortable talking about things so close to my home and family."*

> *"I'm not able to comment about that at this time. Would you mind if we moved on to something else?"*

Whatever you do decide to say, do not freak out and remember to breath. Be as honest as you can without giving away the farm, because even a half way decent reporter can usually tell if you're hiding something and you don't want that.

The kind of polite hedging that I'm suggesting puts the onus back on the reporter and they can either choose to respect your boundaries or not. This also forces the reporter to work a little harder and come up with a more clever way of getting you to respond.

Keep in mind when you're throwing up these kinds of

roadblocks - always do it in a polite and friendly way. The alternative is for you or your publicist to lay down some ground rules in advance of the interview. Some members of the media will agree to ground rules and others will have no part of it.

If you can't talk about something for legal reasons let the media know beforehand. Tell them that you won't be able to address a specific topic. You can even apologize for it. But don't be surprised if you get a firecracker of a reporter or interviewer on your hands and you wind up talking about it anyway and giving them a scoop. This usually happens when you genuinely like the person and feel that they won't manhandle your message.

I've done lots of interviews where the person I was talking to couldn't talk about a specific issue or event for legal reasons, and that was fine because I knew going into it they weren't going to spill the beans with me. So I just had them go on-the-record by saying, "I can't comment for legal reasons." Case in point, when I talked to Jennifer Lopez the week of the Sean Combs trial, I knew going into it she wasn't going to talk about the trial or Puffy or their relationship, but I also knew I wouldn't be doing my job if I didn't get her to say *something* about it. So, I was quite happy just to have her go on the record saying "For legal reasons I'm unable to comment ... "

Now half the journalists I know will be OK with you and your team putting up these kinds of roadblocks. The other half will throw up their arms in complete disgust. It all depends on how important it is to you and how important it is to them.

"I just try to be honest and keep a "zone" of privacy. It's not my goal in life to be a better interview, that's your problem." ★ Candice Bergen

What If The Reporter Continues?

"You can always choose not to answer a question." ★ Meg Ryan

Oh, we reporters are such a brutal lot and God knows we do love a good cat-fight every now and then, so here's what you do if your relentless reporter won't relent.

Calmly, and I say it with a capitol "C," repeat what you already said (see above). Or, say something like, "I understand why you need to ask me this, but I make it a rule not to discuss those kinds of issues/subjects/topics publicly." Absolutely tell the truth when you say this.

Do it calmly and in a sporting way. But don't sweat it too much because that sneaky little reporter knows exactly what he or she is doing, and what they're doing is looking to grab a headline or a scoop ... it's what they do for a living. So, it's totally up to you to determine if you want to give it to them or not. Above all, do not lose your cool under any circumstances. To do so would be like pouring gasoline on a fire.

And remember you're there to get your story out there. If you don't want to be interviewed and don't want to be there, it's a waste of time.

What If The Journalist Starts Badgering Me For Answers? What Do I Do Then?

"They'll just wait till you're tired to set up to destroy your reputation. There's always somebody that decides they're gonna make a living chewing on your bones." ★ James Woods

I know it's hard to believe that a journalist might get a little wacky on you, but if a member of the press continues harping on you - to the point that you're just plain uncomfortable - then stop the interview right then and there. Just don't go storming out of the room. Keep your cool and be polite, if you still can. You might try saying something like, "I'd like to stop now, if you don't mind. I think we have different goals here and I don't think either of us are reaching ours."

www.GaylMurphy.com

Above all, be gracious, it's a small world. You never know when you may have to face this person again and you want to keep this all on the up and up. In the words of Michael Corleone, "It's not personal, Sonny. It's strictly business."

"The press is unequivocally the enemy - just be as nice to them as you can." ★ *James Woods*

PART FOUR:

LET'S GET TECHNICAL!

PART FOUR:

LET'S GET TECHNICAL!

What's All This About Soundbites?

"Sometimes we just sound so ridiculous, don't we? When we are talking about what we do."
★ *Laura San Giacomo*

Ah, soundbites, the manna the media thrives on! Those little golden bites of story and information that are snapshots of your life – soundbites reveal who you are, what you've got going on and what you're selling.

In print, a soundbite is a quote. In electronic media, it's called a soundbite. A soundbite is also your pitch or your tag all dressed up and ready for a night on the town!

A soundbite is a brief and outstanding mini-version of who you are and/or whatever it is you're selling, in twenty seconds or less.

A soundbite is also a complete thought, full of color and detail and delivered in the shortest amount of time.

Delivering soundbites isn't a race ... it just feels like one.

A soundbite can be something as simple as a reaction to a headline, or why your product will save the world. It can even be something as mundane as your favorite vacation spot.

A great soundbite is full of energy and is pithy, colorful, funny or thoughtful ... In fact, at times it's a combination of all these things.

MURPHY'S LAW

A Really Great Soundbite Is Both ... The Sizzle And The Steak!

Great Soundbites Throughout History!

"You like me, you really, really like me." ★ Sally Field

"Frankly my dear, I don't give a damn!" ★ Rhett Butler

"I'll be back ..." ★ T-800 (The Terminator)

"I have a dream!" ★ Martin Luther King Jr.

"May the Force be with you!" ★ Ben (Obi-Wan) Kenobi

"You gotta be really careful what you bite off. Don't bite off more than you can chew." ★ Ozzy Osbourne

"Let my people go!" ★ Moses

"Read my lips, no new taxes!" ★ George W. Bush Sr.

"Follow your bliss." ★ Joseph Campbell

"I did not have sex with that woman." ★ Bill Clinton

"I have always depended upon the kindness of strangers!" ★ Blanche DuBois

"Life is what happens when you're busy making other plans!" ★ John Lennon

"Go ahead, make my day!" ★ "Dirty" Harry Callahan

"If you have to spend money on marketing, then you're doing something wrong!" ★ *TheMarketingMan.com*

"I'm not a ham, I'm the whole pig!" ★ *Paul Stanley (KISS)*

"A record company is like a giant ATM machine ..." ★ *Beck*

"You gotta tell it to sell it!" ★ *Gayl Murphy*

How many famous quotes or soundbites can you think of?

MURPHY'S LAW

One of the most important aspects of meeting the press without getting clobbered is knowing what soundbites are and knowing how to identify them and how to use them in a media friendly way.

And the best way to accomplish this is by doing some homework! It's workbook time again ... Start by watching the media at its commercial best and that means carefully scrutinizing TV shows, listening to radio programs and reading the kinds of magazines that are most likely to be interested enough in you to want to talk to you.

Begin by watching, listening and studying exactly what feeds the publicity media machine. Programs and networks like CNN, *Entertainment Tonight*, *Access Hollywood*, The Cooking Channel, *The Today Show*, talk shows and tech shows, FOX News, MSNBC and the like. Be aware that every time the camera cuts to the person who's being interviewed and you actually hear that person speak ... *that's a soundbite!*

In a pre-produced program like the evening news, A&E's *Biography* or VH1's *Behind the Music* ... those "interview bites" are "produced soundbites" and were specifically chosen for air because they fit the producer's storyline and show criteria.

You can even watch or listen to these programs with a stopwatch and time these soundbites. You'll be amazed at how long 17 seconds is and how much information people can cram into just seven. You can start by using a small hand-held tape recorder and taping these programs for soundbites. And in doing so, you'll get familiar with what soundbites really *sound* like. Or, you can use the *Soundbites That Grab Me* section located in *Part Three* of the *Interview Tactics Workbook* at the back of the book and write them in yourself. (See page 131)

A word of caution here for you aspiring media stars ... if you don't get a good handle on soundbites, no matter what you've accomplished in your career, you're in for a bit of a rocky ride.

Again, I am not in any way suggesting, that everything that comes out of your mouth has to be some sort of neat or cutesy morsel. I'm just saying that the electronic media thrives on this type of clean and neat sound, so it's best that you add soundbites to your bag of media tricks, *even if you only have one starting out.*

If this "finding your soundbite" business is daunting to you and you're not getting it right away, try going back over your *talking points*. Armed with what you now know about soundbites, try making some up. (See page 135)

Dressing For An Interview!

"I'm ready for my close-up, Mr. DeMille."
★ *Norma Desmond in Sunset Boulevard*

Bathing and clean clothes is always advisable. As for what you should wear, I always advise dressing the way you want to be described in the piece or remembered on the show.

If you're a musician, artist, actor, actress, nutty professor, designer or someone who wants to be known for their unique sense of style, in the words of David Crosby, "Let your freak flag fly!" Don't hide those dreadlocks or that 44DD cleavage. And, if it's not sunny inside, you may want to rethink the sunglasses.

MURPHY'S LAW

Always Dress For Success ... And, Dress For Business. Whatever Your Business Happens To Be!

If your doing a TV interview or a photo shoot and you happen to be a clothing designer or jewelry designer, do yourself a favor and wear, or bring along one of your creations or ensembles. If you're a chef, try wearing your apron so the audience can visualize you in the kitchen. Have you ever seen Wolfgang Puck do an interview on TV? The guy always looks like he flew right out of the kitchen at that exact moment just to do the interview. Getting the point? I mean have you ever seen Norm Abrams from *This Old House* wearing a suit and tie? Never! The idea is to put yourself into the picture without going overboard. Just be you!

Depending on what your gig is, think about your image; think about what your wardrobe and personal style says about you. Even if you buy just one outfit and wear it only for interviews, it's OK because it's show time!

If you're really uncertain about finding your style, check out the competition. Seek out someone you think expresses a message of personal style that's similar to yours. Find a secret role model, someone successful and who has the style, confidence and grace you'd like to possess and copy what you like about them - just don't become them. Tony Robbins would call this "mirroring." I call it, "stealing from the best!"

"I have fun. This is nothing scary. I mean, there's nothing I have to hide except my fur."
★ *Robin Williams*

In my humble opinion, one of the best examples of someone "stealing from the best," is Madonna. Early in her career, didn't she do an incredible job of "mirroring" Marilyn Monroe? Madonna critics accused "The Material Girl" of ripping Marilyn off, but really all she did was find a secret role model. Madonna's a champion at mirroring. Plus, mirroring is a great skill to have especially when it comes time to reinvent yourself.

On the other side of the mirror, here's what *not* to do … If you're the CEO of a conservative European bank, I don't think it's in your best interest to waltz into the interview decked out like Snoop Dogg, even if he is your "homey," but that's just my opinion.

What Language Is Your Body Speaking?
And What Is It Saying About You?

"I've always been comfortable doing interviews, except when the movie's not that good."
★ *Billy Crystal*

Remember way back, when your mom nagged you to "stop slouching, get your hair out of your face, sit up straight and get your hands out of your pockets"?

Well, your mom told you that because:

A) She was right.
B) Mom's always tell kids stuff like that, and
C) Because she knew the true value of first
   impressions.

Your mom knew from her own experience that **how people see you is how they'll remember you** … so have them remember you as "a nice person."

So where am I going with this? The best advice I can give you about body language is to carry your body like the superstar that you are! Start by:

Standing tall and showing the world that you're happy to be here.

Sitting up straight, looking enthusiastic and don't forget to breathe.

Looking at the person you're talking to and making eye contact. Smile.

Finding your "zone" and hanging out there.

By becoming familiar with your *personal zone*, you'll better be able to figure out what's comfortable for your body and where to place your arms and legs - the mind leads and the body follows.

Also, if you've been thinking about starting a workout program or joining a gym to shed a few pounds because you think it will make you feel better about yourself, do it.

Is It OK To Be Funny?

"Sometimes I've made great friends with journalists. Just because they're asking about me doesn't mean that they're not interesting."
★ *John Lithgow*

Did you hear the one about the reporter who walked into a bar with a duck under his arm?

Yes, it's OK to be funny in an interview especially if it comes naturally to you, or if the story of your rocky road to success happens to be a funny one. It's also OK to be funny if you're Robin Williams or Chris Rock - that's even better. But if being funny doesn't come naturally to you, if it's not *authentically* who you are, I think it's probably best to just stick to the basics ... just don't be a stick in the mud. You can *think* funny.

Keep in mind, what kills on TV isn't a guarantee of belly laughs on radio, or in print. Above all, remember nobody likes a smartass, unless you're Don Rickles. Get a feeling for the mood. If no one is laughing but you - change the channel!

Is There Really Such A Thing As "Off the Record"?

"If you don't have anything nice to say, don't say anything, but sometimes I'll just say, 'Yeah, he was an (expletive).'" ★ Robert Downey Jr.

There are two schools of thought on what's on and what's off the record. One school will agree to it; the other believes there are no sacred cows, ever! This kind of honor system depends solely on the journalist and who they're working for.

In a perfect world, you should be able to say, "Can we talk off the record?" And a journalist *should* be able to honor that by answering yes or no. If you really need to say something to the reporter, you can always ask, "Would you mind turning off the tape or the camera; I'll answer that off the record."

However, if the subject is really sensitive and there are cameras and recorders in the room, you might want to take them outside or suggest meeting at another location.

My personal opinion on this "on-the-record, off-the-record" debate is, why take the chance? You *must assume* that it's ALL on the record, *always.* So be very, very careful how you answer the question, what you say and how you phrase it.

I also don't think it's necessary to tell a complete stranger how you masterminded a bank robbery in 1970 and that you are still a fugitive. Know what I'm saying? Although, if you're feuding with your record label, network, publisher, sponsor or former employer and you want your side of the story out there, go for it, but tread very, very carefully.

It is remarkable the number of times the interviewer has come in with a predetermined point of view." ★ Kelsey Grammer

www.GaylMurphy.com

Not All Interviews Are The Same!

"I like to make people get a slice of who you are for real. Because who they see on the screen is always totally different." ★ *Catherine Zeta-Jones*

For our purposes here in the media jungle, there are three types of interviews:

❶ *Television*
❷ *Radio*
❸ *Print*

The thing to keep in mind is that they're all very different from each other and that's what we need to discuss next.

TV Interviews

Without going through the whole brew-ha-ha about why media meisters think TV is so great, you should know that the majority of the Media-Gods; studio executives, publicists, and talent managers consider television to be "The King of All Media."

Although for our purposes here, the job you're doing is the same regardless of which media you're dealing with because if you can't tell it, you can't sell it. You've got a story that needs to be told and soundbites that need to be delivered. The added bonus of TV is that there's a visual persona of you as well as the audio persona, and that will help you get your story out there.

Amazing Interview Tactics Factoid!

In 1969, the average Presidential TV soundbite was 47 seconds.

In 2001, the average Presidential TV soundbite was only 8 seconds!

---

www.InterviewTactics.com

On a television newscast or newsmagazine show, your soundbite probably won't exceed 10 seconds, unless you're Steven Spielberg, an alien from a foreign galaxy, having sex with the President (again) or you just found the *Missing Link*. When you're doing an interview for TV, it's always a challenge, so *don't focus on delivering soundbites.* Focus on the questions and telling *your story.*

If you know your story and how to tell it, you're coming from an authentic place inside yourself and you've done the *Interview Tactics Workbook*, believe me, those adorable little soundbites will just pop right out of your mouth. As a matter of fact, your soundbites will probably end up delivering themselves and you'll have more answers than you'll know what to do with.

It's important to remember time flies on-the-air, and that you've got to know how to cut to the chase at a moment's notice - because many times that's all you're going to get - is a couple of moments. Sure, you were booked for a three-minute interview, but by the time they finally get to you, your time's been whittled down to 60 seconds!

So, now you've got to figure out how to get your story out there in a minute instead of three! What that means is you have to put your listening skills (for what's being said) to the test. You've got to know which part of your story is appropriate (in the time allotted) and get to the point.

The best way to get to the point is to have several different versions of your story ready and to be prepared to use them. Part Four of the *Interview Tactics Workbook* was specifically created to help you uncover all of these gems. (See page 135)

The 15-Second Version:

"I invented Chinese Food in A Bag for Chung Pao Shrimp addicts everywhere. It's my version of Cantonese 'brown bagging' it ... blah, blah, blah."

The Two-Minute Version:

"Back in 1996, when my wife and I first got married we moved to Milwaukee. She was still in collage and I was working in a Chinese restaurant ... blah, blah, blah."

Think back to the last time you called a friend with some hot gossip and they couldn't talk to you. What did they say? It was probably something like, "Talk fast, I've gotta go." It's amazing how many juicy and colorful details you were able to cram into that compressed amount of time. You wanted five minutes, they gave you two and you were able to get your whole story in. Got it? Get it? Just don't get clobbered!

So, if your time does get cut, and it probably will, don't take it personally, that's showbiz folks. Your job in this situation is to **stay focused on your story** and your *talking points*, listening and answering the questions, and knowing that a good reporter can take your 60-second answer and pull three great soundbites out of it. So, stay with telling and selling your story ... whichever version you choose to tell.

MURPHY'S LAW

One of the biggest mistakes Media Virgins make is thinking the interview is just about them ... *it's not!*

PART FIVE:

THIS IS WHERE IT GETS GOOD!
"HURRAY FOR HOLLYWOOD!"

www.InterviewTactics.com

PART FIVE:

THIS IS WHERE IT GETS GOOD! *"HURRAY FOR HOLLYWOOD!"*

"I don't really want to be 'got', that's why I don't do television interviews." ★ *Jack Nicholson*

Questions You Get To Ask During The Set Up Of Your TV Interview

Did you know you're allowed to ask questions going into a TV interview? Well, you are and here's a little appetizer of what you might consider asking:

"Is there something specific you'd like me to talk about?"

"What outlet is it for?"

"Where and when is the interview airing?"

"Are you shooting indoors or outdoors?"

"How much time do you need?"

"Should I bring samples of my work with me? The book, the cookie, the award, the painting, the artifact, the car?"

If they're coming to your home turf to shoot, you can ask:

"Does it need to be 'studio quiet'?"

"What type of room do you want to shoot in?"

"Are they looking for a specific background?"

You'll find the answers to these questions helpful in determining how you want to appear on camera. For instance, if you just caught the world's biggest fish or Barry Bonds' record-breaking homer, you might consider co-starring the fish, if it's not too stinky or wearing an A's cap and showing off the ball.

Smile For The Camera!

"Once you're on film (or video), there's no more room for interpretation. There you sit." ★ Jack Nicholson

When you do a TV interview the better you look on camera, the better the interview will look. So, I hereby give you permission to "doll up," just don't go overboard unless you're a Las Vegas showgirl, Dame Edna or Bjork. And, if you really want the camera person to love you, I suggest that you not wear solid white, unless you're a nurse, doctor, scientist or lab technician and they're shooting you at work.

If you're doing a lengthy TV interview and it rolls into a second or third day, do you think that has an impact on your wardrobe? You bet it does, especially if you're the subject of a documentary, and it's "a day in the life." Talk to your producer because they probably want you to wear the same clothes all three days for continuity. So be aware.

When choosing your wardrobe, think about **how you want the world to see you**. In my humble opinion, it's best to dress the part - whatever your part is - and dress for success!

Take your cues from the pros. Michael Jordan is a great media superstar to "mirror." Jordan always looks impeccable, successful and ready to do business. I don't recall ever hearing anything negative about him based on his appearance or how he deals with the media.

As a matter of fact, he's so keenly aware of his role model status, especially with young people - and that one picture is worth a thousand words - most in the media already know that when Michael shows up, he'll be looking fabulous, suited up and it's business as usual.

Don't kid yourself, the public and the media *will* make snap judgments about you based on how you look on TV, so choose a look that's right for you and for what you're selling and commit to it. If you're a guy with a five o'clock shadow or you're a gal with a ring through your nose, be aware that it's these things that telegraph your message to the world.

So, if that's who you are in real life and that's how you want the world to know you, then I say, "Go for it, Baby."

What The Heck *Is* All This Stuff?

So there you are, all dressed up, ready to tell it to sell it, and you're surrounded by all this stuff. What then? Whatever you do, don't let the confusion of the set, the camera, lights and sound equipment throw you.

The people standing around looking very TV-like are probably the interviewer/reporter, producer, a sound person and/or a production assistant. What's really going on here is that *you're* visiting *them* in *their* office, even if they're shooting in yours.

These people you see moving your furniture around do this everyday of the week - and the hubbub of the lights and sound are just another day at the office for them. So don't get nervous.

Let the reporter, interviewer or producer take the lead when it comes to where you should sit or stand and what's in the background of the shot. Although, if you have a gorgeous city view, a wall full of awards or a waterfall in your backyard, you might want to bring that to their attention.

When it comes to dealing with the camera, and this goes for all TV interviews, ask the reporter or producer where they would like you to look. Some will want you to look directly into the camera lens and some won't, so ask. Also, be prepared to have your microphone clipped onto your shirt or hot wired up your blouse. Be aware that the person who's doing the clipping should know not to attach it to your leather jacket or near a jingling chain because of the noise factor. If they don't, be a smart little cookie and mention it.

While doing the interview, you might notice that the interviewer is noticeable quiet or silently responding, or his or her questions are lagging behind your answers.

Don't let this throw you. What it usually means is the person interviewing you isn't necessarily the person that will be included in the produced piece. They may be doing the interview for another reporter and they can't have their voice on the track or they want your soundbites to "stand alone."

Just know that when your interviewer is not talking to you in "real time," quite often that means they're either going for a "clean sound" or they've got some production trick up their sleeve that you don't need to concern yourself with.

You can also ask if there's something special they would like you to talk about, or if it's just a straight "Q&A." For example, if you just won a Grammy for yodeling, do yourself a favor and ask if they want a demonstration.

This kind of teamwork will make you look smarter and will endear you to the media. Believe it or not, you may actually see the reporter or producer sigh with relief. And that's a good thing.

Once the interview wraps, they may have you stay a minute or two longer so they can shoot around you or shoot the reporter doing some "reactions shots."

What this usually means is, they only have one camera and they want some additional footage to cut to for the piece.

Remember the crying scene in *Broadcast News*? Just like that ... except there will be no tears in your feature piece.

Remotes Aren't About Control, Or "What Do You Mean I Have To Sit In A Room By Myself?"

Once you've booked your TV interview you should know that not all interviewers or chat shows are able to "shoot" you in person. Sometimes they'll be in another city, state or country and you have to go to a TV studio or some other remote location to be interviewed. This is called "doing a remote or a satellite tour." And, no matter how seasoned you are at interacting with the media, doing "remote interviews" can be about as weird as it gets.

Remote interviews involve you sitting in a room, looking into a camera and listening to the questions through a tiny earpiece called an IFB. So basically, there you are, sitting in a chair, alone in a room with a thing stuck in one ear, carrying on a conversation with a $20,000 camera. Baffling? Yes. Impossible? Not at all.

The trick to pulling off a killer remote interview is pretending that the person you're talking to is right there with you in the studio. You can also imagine the face of a friend or a role model in the center of the camera lens and you're telling them your story. This kind of pretending takes lots of concentration, but you got to where you're at right now by concentration and focus, so just call upon that part of yourself and dive right in.

It might also be helpful to you to find out how much time you have going into the interview so that you can decide which part of your story you're going to tell ... the epic novel or the *Reader's Digest* version? You can ask the producer what questions they will be asking - so you can prep a little - and nine times out of ten they'll tell you. Also, feel free to add your two cents by updating them in the event you just received some kind of award or recognition.

Remember to relax and let the helpful people who work in the studio give you the information you need to know. And, if you're really nice, they'll even offer you water or coffee!

When your remote interview is over and the folks on the other end say that the interview turned out well, no matter how you felt about it ... if they say it was good, then it went well.

Press Junkets And Roundtables

One hundred plus reporters all asking the same questions? Gosh that doesn't sound very probing or journalistic. What's going on in the media jungle and how did this happen?

Once upon a time around 1990, several natives got together in the marketing and PR department of an unnamed Hollywood studio and started to brainstorm. They decided the next time they had a movie to pitch, their talent would do interviews in a production line format. Hence the birth of the "press junket." There were press junkets way before this, but they were very different. These natives decided this "press junket" idea would be a public relations bonanza ... and what a bang they could get for their marketing bucks! And they were right on both counts.

Recently I've noticed that publishing houses are starting to get into the act as well, so you authors out there ... listen up. Having been to more junkets than I can shake a press kit at, I can tell you with authority, press junkets can sometimes be more of a western-style roundup than an *inner-view* ... *"Yee-ha, head 'em up and move 'em out, pardner."*

So what *is* a press junket and how exactly does it work? A press junket usually takes place in hotel over several days and it's an ongoing series of press interviews that can include as many as a hundred media outlets, reporters and journalists from TV, print, radio and online. In most cases, these interviews are conducted in a production-line format with the various outlets doing their interviews in the same room, asking questions in 20 minutes or less. Now, that's print, radio and online. TV gets talent one-on-one for 3 to 5 minutes. And, if you happened to be the talent ... what then?

www.GaylMurphy.com

For a TV press junket, you're usually set up in a posh hotel suite that's converted into a studio, and one by one each press person is brought in to interview you for three to five minutes, sort of like a PR version of musical chairs. And yes, each person is timed down to the second. Studios and publicists like the idea that their talent can be interviewed by dozens of press outlets over two days, rather than 25 outlets in two weeks. And that's the upside. So keep your answers sicsinct, to the point and no tangents please.

And the down side of press junkets? As a journalist? ... gee ... I dunno, you tell me?

Roundtable Interviews

"I prefer round table (radio and print) interviews to the one-on-one (TV) interviews. They're unbearable and it's no one's fault." ★ *Tim Robbins*

Radio, print and online interviews are affectionately referred to as *roundtables*, and they're not that different from TV one-on-ones in the sense that - yes, they're also like a western roundup, but at least radio and print will get to spend *some* time with you. Twenty minutes as opposed to three to five minutes with TV. I've actually done TV interviews where they told me, while I was walking into the room, that my time had been cut to two minutes! Can you believe that?

Roundtable interviews work like this: reporters (as many as twenty) are seated around an actual *roundtable* and one by one the press ask you questions. Sort of like a well-oiled mini-press conference except everyone is seated at the same *roundtable*. When the allotted time is up, it's you who's moved to another room with another *roundtable* and the process begins again, in increments of 20 minutes or less. In some cases, there can be as many as eight to ten *roundtable* in a four-hour period. Radio and print *roundtables* can be grueling for obvious reasons, so get lots of sleep the night before and don't forget to take your vitamins.

When you first sit down at a one-on-one interview or a *roundtable*, be mindful of the microphone so that you can talk directly into it without obsessing on it. Let the interviewer adjust your microphone for you. And a word of advise: no gum, no sucking candy, no squishing candy wrappers, no food, no clinking ice cubes in your diet cola and no need to grab at the microphone and pretend you're Eminem, or that you're holding a press conference at the White House. It's amazing how many celebrities do that. (I'm not telling.) Make sure you're sitting comfortably and then just start chatting. You can start by saying, "How are you?" Or, "How about those Lakers?"

Radio Interviews

"Radio is a whole different ball game because you can really communicate with the people."
★ Arnold Schwarzenegger

Ah, radio ... my favorite medium. Having been in radio most of my career, I can tell you with great authority that the people who say they love radio, just don't love radio ... they *LOVE* radio*!*

Steve Martin loves radio, Jack Nicholson won't do television interviews, but he'll do radio interviews and then there's Russell Crowe who's just plain nutty about radio, truly! Russell Crowe LOVES being interviewed for radio so much that when he does *roundtables* in L.A., he locks the door so his interview isn't over till he says it is - which is basically unheard of in the media jungle. His little act of defiance drives studio publicists crazy and how fun for a reporter is that?

When Russell did his press interviews for *The Insider*, he drove the studio PR people up a wall because he wouldn't unlock the door and he wouldn't come out of the radio room until he decided his interview was over. Truly, they couldn't get him out. The studio knocked and knocked but he wouldn't unlock the door. They wound up calling security for the key and forcing the door open.

At the interviews for *Mystery, Alaska* and *Beautiful Mind*, Russell was up to his tricks there too, locking doors, chasing away publicists and not coming out. But at the *Proof Of Life* interviews, of all people, it was Sandra Bullock who convinced him to wrap it up. Bullock, it seems, was scheduled to use the room after him for her interviews for *Miss Congeniality* and Russell's door locking tactics was putting her behind schedule. So she barged in and ordered him right out. (Personally, I thought that was the best scene in the movie ... Oh, it wasn't *in* the movie?)

So why do people love radio so much? I think it's because radio is the fuzzy, snuggly in your ear medium and in radio, it all happens in the listener's head. I could go on and on about my love for Marconi's brainstorm, but that'll be my next book.

When you're doing a radio interview, it is important to remember that your level of performance (not your energy) is considerably less than it is with a TV interview. And that's because you're basically just having a conversation with another person. You're talking and they're listening, but you both are working.

Anyone Can "Wrap"

"So here we have to talk in kind of complete sentences. Is that the idea? And repeat your question ... should I do that too?"
★ *Arnold Schwarzenegger*

Be sure you listen carefully to a reporter's questions so your answers can be wrapped around their questions. Here are some examples - bad and good - of wrapping answers around questions, or incorporating questions into answers:

Bad Wrapping:

Q - "How is it that you were able to decipher the Dead Sea Scrolls?"

A - *"Very carefully."*

Good Wrapping:

Q - "How is it that you were able to decipher the Dead Sea Scrolls?"

A - *"I was able to decipher the Dead Sea Scrolls using an X-ray vision machine in my basement. I got the idea after reading about Keith Moon."*

Q - "When did you first realize you could paint like Michelangelo?"

A - *"Actually, it was my parents that first realized that I could paint like Michelangelo. As a matter of fact they tell this really funny story about when I was three years old and I'd paint on the walls ... blah blah blah."*

By incorporating or wrapping their questions in *your* answers, you're giving your interviewer a jumping off point for their next question.

Now they can ask you that funny story you were talking about. You've given them information they can use and work with. Once again you've given them a place to go next.

MURPHY'S LAW

Incorporating the questions into your answers is not exclusive to radio interviews. Wrapping works like a charm in ANY interview!

Usually radio soundbites won't exceed 15 seconds, but the same rules apply as before.

Relax, enjoy, breathe, have energy and your story it will deliver itself! A good reporter or producer can edit around you with no trouble at all.

www.GaylMurphy.com

Getting Ready For Radio

*"Of course (the press will) criticize, because that's what they do." ★ Lance Bass (*NSYNC)*

If the reporter is coming to your office or home, it's mandatory that you provide them with a quiet place. A room with a table is always a nice touch so they can set up a mike stand and their tape recorder.

MURPHY'S LAW

As with *all* interviews, *turn off your phones ... office phone, cell phone, fax machine, pager or anything else you can think of that chirps, beeps, rings, burps or otherwise makes noise on its own.*

No pet noises either unless you're an animal trainer, or your Iguana talks. And no kids, unless they've won an Oscar or the lottery. If you're the world's fastest talker, ask your interviewer if they want to record you speed talking.

If you're a singer/songwriter, ask if they want an acoustic performance. Remember, a reporter doesn't have all the answers and it's your interview too - and this is supposed to be fun. So strut your stuff and don't forget to share your goodies because it makes good radio. In the words of Mama Rose, "Smile, Baby."

Radio Remotes And Radio Tours

"You know we're in a business where we want people to have a good time, so you should tell them about it." ★ Kurt Russell

Not all radio interviews require that the reporter, interviewer, or show host be in person with you, same as TV. Many times you'll be booked for an interview from another city, state or country, in which case you'll either do your interview over the phone from your home or hotel room or from a broadcast facility using ISDN lines or satellite.

This kind of interview is called a *remote interview*, a *2-way*, a *phoner* or a *radio tour*."

Radio tours, like TV tours, are a really great marketing and PR tool because you can hit dozens of markets in just a few of hours. You get to sit in a cushy studio or hotel room, drinking coffee and just talking to radio stations "live" on the air, one right after the other. Each interview should take five to ten minutes; they're punchy and fun to do. Two-ways and radio tours almost always transcend radio format from station to station and market to market. This means one interview might be with an FM classic rocker, the next with an AM all-talk station and the third with some whacked-out morning show.

It's those whacked-out morning radio shows that I want to focus on right now. And that's because if you don't possess the moxie of a Rosie O'Donnell or you're aren't prepared to do battle while you strut your stuff, you could be knocked right out of your *zone* doing one of these high profile morning shows and never know how it happened!

Regardless of what you think about these incredibly popular and successful morning shows, they're the real moneymakers for most radio stations. They pull in more revenue than any other day part ... and in most cases can get away with more crazy and mean-spirited stuff than any other shows on that station. The last thing I want for you, as a result of being interviewed on this type of show, is that you get clobbered by them. So how can you prepare to successfully give a killer interview on one of these wild and crazy morning shows?

Let me start by saying that I have the greatest respect for anyone that makes a living in radio, but that doesn't mean that I agree with some the shtick that got them there. Because at the end of the day, if you're a woman, a lot of these morning crews are just gonna want to know if you're wearing panties.

www.GaylMurphy.com

And if you're a guy, they wanna know if you "got some" last night. Now not all morning shows are like this, just a lot of the really successful ones. So, if you have any second thoughts about doing these shows, here are some hints to help you make up your mind:

Call anyone you know that might know anything about the show and ask about it. Tell them you're trying to determine the vibe of the show and how they're known for handling their guests.

Call a relative or a friend that lives in that city and ask them about the show.

Call the entertainment editor of the local newspaper in that city and ask them what the deal is ... friend or foe?

Call the station while the show is on the air and ask to be put on hold. You'll get to hear the program over the phone and you can listen and judge for yourself.

Print ... The *Windy* Medium

"I know you've got an article to write so I've got to be somewhat quotable and a little bit pithy."
★ Ray Liotta

Print reporters, unlike radio and TV reporters don't usually care about soundbites per say, although if you lay a really good one on them they'll be the first to scoop it up.

What print reporters really want from you is that you speak in complete sentences, no matter how long your sentences happen to be. If they're really fragmented, or a series of Neanderthal-like grunts, there's a good chance they're gonna think you're not the sharpest tool in the shed. So, speak up, keep your energy up, stay focused and talk in complete sentences. If you can do that, at least you'll be in the ballpark.

MURPHY'S LAW

No "One-Word" Answers ... And Especially No "Yes or No" Answers! [This applies to ALL types of interviews!]

For print interviews you need to elaborate on your answers and give details using examples.

When you're being interviewed for print it's perfectly OK to pause and take your time and think about your answers, especially if you're doing a one-on-one interview and have some time to spend. Most interviewers I know are usually fine with this. You can even say, "Can you give me a minute to think about that?" Or, "Can we come back to that?" And make sure you do.

The secret of feature print reporters ... They want to know what makes you tick!

For example, let's say your company just invented a home unit that allows you to track your spouse using cable TV. (Hey, I'm not judging you.) So, what a featured print reporter might want to know, in addition to how the darn thing works, is:

When did you decide to create your little super snooper?

Was snooping something you thought a lot about when you were a kid?

Have you ever won any prizes for your detective techniques?

As a kid, did your family encourage you to spy on your sisters and brothers?

If so, what were they doing? And did they sneak up on you as well?

www.GaylMurphy.com

This is the sort of background information and minutia that is delicious in print. Print reporters build stories, and they want to go right to the source, paint the picture and drop you in it. So, be a bud and give them the goods.

Think Color, Think Detail And Be Specific!

My dear friend veteran writer/reporter Luaine Lee, who writes for Scripps Howard News Service, is such a stickler for detail that she's of the mind that *specificity* is the single most important ingredient to keep in mind when being interviewed for print. If you're an actor and Luaine is interviewing you and you say you were bitten by the acting bug when you were in a play at school, she'll want to know what grade you were in, what the play was, the name of your character, what your costume looked like and who made it!

Luaine tells a sweet story about when she did the interviews for Steven's Spielberg's *A.I.* and she noticed that young Haley Joel Osment was not only wearing patent leather shoes, but that one of his laces was untied. Which to me was no big deal, but for her it was that single untied lace that most captured the essence of Haley Joel.

On the one hand, you have this young self confidant actor who was 13 going on 35, mature and poised with the media. And, on the other, he's a kid just being a kid with his untied shoelaces telling the tale. No matter how you slice it and dice it, according to Luaine, he's just one of millions of boys all over the world who just can't keep his shoelaces tied!

Press Conferences And The Red Carpet

"I can conduct myself on the Red Carpet, but I can tell you it is not my favorite place to be ..."
★ *Kevin Costner*

Press conferences and the Red Carpet are basically just another forum for giving a killer interview. As a matter of fact, if you haven't figured it out yet, everywhere you go is an opportunity for you tell your story. How many times have you heard about a reporter who stumbled upon an expert, celebrity or a newsmaker at the car wash and came away with a scoop or a great story? Plenty ... so don't get bent out of shape because of the location of an interview.

Press Conferences

A press conference is a great way to meet the press when you've got an important time sensitive announcement to make. A press conference can be scheduled to announce the release of your latest movie, book, award, the opening of your new corporate headquarters, the debut of your newest line of clothing, cosmetic line or the opportunity to tell your side of the story ... and so on. You get the picture?

Most of the questions you'll be asked will be about whatever you're announcing, so it's important that you really know your stuff before you set foot in front of the microphones and cameras. Because if you don't ... you *will* get clobbered!

A press conference is usually set up by your publicist, or the PR department of the company, so you probably don't need to sweat the details of the event. You've seen enough press conferences on TV and in the movies to know that you'll be either sitting or standing at a podium and you'll be face to face with a room of journalists and reporters and one by one they'll be shouting out questions to you. Watch President George W. Bush, Jr. in a press conference situation. He's a master at it. He makes every reporter feel special and that no question is stupid. He's great at this. He takes his time, looks every reporter in the eye and he goes from one to the next and the next and so on. He's confident and it shows in his body language, because he knows his material. And, he also knows he's surrounded by gang of experts that will come to his aid in a nanosecond.

The single thing to remember when doing a press conference

is not to be nervous - you asked these people to be there and it's your room ... so work it. And, answer the questions in an open and honest way.

Tell your story so that *they* can tell your story. Give the facts, then back them up with the details. Take them to that place ...

... just don't buy any real estate there. In other words, get to the point. Relax, take your time and allow the confidence you feel for your products and services to shine through.

The Red Carpet

For everything you've seen and heard about The Red Carpet, at the end of the day it's really nothing more than a rolled up rug. It's what goes on that carpet, that could potentially get you clobbered, like an evil magic carpet ride. The Red Carpet, or *Arrivals*, is in fact an actual stretch of carpet that extends from either the street to the front entrance of a hotel or concert hall, or from inside the front entrance to a ballroom or cocktail reception. And on both sides of this long carpet is a line of lots and lots of press ... each competing for a minute or two, or three from you. *Arrivals* is usually all-media including the paparazzi. You can always tell where the photographers are because they're the most vocal. You can hear them from a block away. What happens while you're on the Red Carpet is that you'll be led by a "handler" who will take you from outlet to outlet for a minute or two and then you'll slowly move on and do it all over again.

Doing interviews on the Red Carpet can take a lot more time and it can be a lot more work than you think, so it's advisable, if you want to be perky, that you grab a protein bar or quick snack beforehand. At the Oscars and the Grammys, it can take as long as an hour to get from the car to the front entrance because of all the media ... and that's a lot of yakkin.' It's a media assembly line and you're the one that's moving.

The Red Carpet is a soundbite festival. It's quick loud Q&A

and it's best that you have lots of energy and be ready to play a little ... just don't be too cute, it's not worth it. You're there to get some morsel of your story out to the media. Stay within the confines of why you're there and try and have some fun around your message. It's unlikely that any of the questions will be too probing, although you never want to rule anything out. But when that reporter at the premier of *Toy Story* asks you about *your* favorite toy as a kid ... absolutely tell them about that stuffed pony.

It's also a good idea beforehand to go over what your upcoming projects are because you'll probably be asked about them. Be prepared and remember, you can always bring this stuff up yourself. If you don't have anything firm yet, phrase it in such a way that you don't sound like a dud. Above all, just don't lie.

Press Conferences and the Red Carpet can really be daunting. They're noisy and unruly and there's usually tons of people shouting and hanging around all over the place, and it's really easy to get distracted ... but don't. That's not to say you shouldn't have fun, have all the fun you can stand. Just remember, stay focused. You're there to tell your story to the world ... and in some cases, the whole world will be watching ... so smile!

The "Media Darling" And How To Become One!

"The media has been in very many ways good to me, especially being a black woman." ★ *Halle Berry*

MURPHY'S LAW

A *Media Darling* is someone the press loves to write and talk about whenever they can.

Sometimes the press falls hopelessly in a love with a celebrity, inventor, artist, politician, entrepreneur, athlete or newsmaker, and it's that person they all want to talk about. The press loves reporting on them so much that it almost doesn't matter if they have something current to sell or not. *Media darlings* are just plain fun to write and talk about, and not necessarily in a tabloid way. So, why not become a *media darlings* and get the whole world talking about you?

Media darlings are people who are so genuinely grateful for what they've accomplished that it's almost subatomic ... to the point that you can almost smell it.

Media darlings have a quality and air about them that is so authentic and so natural that once you've been in the company of these people, you can't help but want to talk about them.

Rudy Giuliani, Salma Hayek, Tony Blair, Bono, George Clooney, Mark McGwire, Colin Powell, Carlos Santana, Kobe Bryant, Jennifer Aniston, Tom Hanks, John Glenn, Steven Tyler, Cher, Bill Clinton, Tiger Woods, Ted Turner, Oprah Winfrey, Senator John McCain, Bill Gates and John Travolta are great examples of *media darlings*. How many more can you think of?

Salma Hayek is a *media darling* because she's honest, effervescent, sexy and really smart. All the *media darlings* I've mentioned are truly a delight to talk to and that's great, because the press *loves* really successful people who speak from their gratitude when they're talking about their lives and their success. And, who could have worked harder on hitting golf balls than Tiger Woods? Surely you've seen those adorable photos of Baby Tiger, out there on the golf course at two-years old? And you know Carlos Santana never thought for a second that his career would span 30 plus years in huge arenas or that he would win armfuls of Grammys.

The reason why Salma Hayek is such good example of a *media darling* is that her personal story is not only compelling and colorful, but she can *really* tell it in a way that makes the interviewer feel important. She weaves her tale with energy and enthusiasm, wit and intelligence. When you first hear her tell her story about having a successful acting career in Mexico and setting her sights on America and making her dream come true, it's as if it's the first time she's ever told it to anyone and she's chosen you be her witness!

The main quality of a *Media Darling* is that they interact with the press in an authentic way.

Media darlings are not afraid to be real, but they don't give away the farm either. They're just delightful to talk to that reporters just write about them whenever they get the chance. I think that's because a genuine *media darling* makes a reporter's job that more fun and also because the public loves to hear about them.

ALMOST
THERE!

ALMOST THERE!

"Take the time to be as articulate as you can be. The art is to not get upset about what they've asked." ★ John Travolta

I couldn't have said this better, had I said it myself. Earlier in *Interview Tactics*, John Travolta talked about coming from your "smarter self."

Hopefully, if you've been following along you now have a handle on who that person "inside of you" is and how to befriend them in an interview situation so that you can ... **tell it to sell it**.

Here's a quick review of *How To Survive The Media Without Getting Clobbered*:

☑ Be as honest as you can with the person who's interviewing you.

☑ Speak authentically and from your *zone*.

☑ Remember, the press is not your enemy unless you did something really, really bad - in which case maybe you should have your attorney with you.

☑ Relax, enjoy and have a good time. Being interviewed is supposed to be fun. You get to be the star of "The Me Show," starring Me (or in this case, You).

☑ No "one word" answers EVER!

☑ Think detail, think color, think story!

www.InterviewTactics.com

☑ Whether you're doing TV, print or radio, have energy.

☑ Telling your story isn't a monologue, so remember to pause and breathe.

☑ Be sure to make eye contact.

☑ Be as specific as you can without being long-winded.

☑ If you're doing an electronic interview, don't wear or bring anything that jingles, beeps, vibrates or otherwise makes noise on it's own.

☑ No sunglasses unless you invented them, you're Bono or it's high noon in the Mojave Desert.

☑ Regardless of what you might think or have been led to believe, the press isn't there to judge you.

☑ Dress for success and how you want the world to know you.

☑ Do not be afraid, but if you are, it's OK to acknowledge it.

☑ You gotta tell it to sell it!

☑ If you were at a party, what is it about you that other people would find fascinating and interesting?

☑ If you're nervous you can say so, just remember this isn't a confessional.

☑ Always answer in complete sentences and "weave" and "wrap" the name of your product, service or project into your answer.

☑ An interview isn't really a conversation, but it's not an interrogation either.

☑ You *can* ask questions.

www.GaylMurphy.com

☑ Talk to a reporter like you're talking to a real, live person.

☑ If you bake cookies, record CDs, grow world-famous flowers or write best selling books, share your goodies.

☑ Check out your body language to make sure you know what it's saying about you.

For the most part, all a reporter really wants is to turn in a great story.

THAT'S A
WRAP!

www.InterviewTactics.com

THAT'S A WRAP!

"Why (do) people know more about actors than the guys who are spending their tax dollars?"
★ *Bruce Willis*

"How do you learn to deal with the loss of anonymity and privacy? You just pray."
★ *Wesley Snipes*

As I was completing the writing of *Interview Tactics: How To Survive The Media Without Getting Clobbered. The Insider's Guide To Giving A Killer Interview*, it occurred to me that perhaps I should say something about the price of fame and the inflated toll it can take on one's privacy under the media microscope since I'm such an ardent cheerleader for the media jungle.

I remember when David Duchovny talked of how he felt about loss of his privacy at the height of his *X-Files* fame. He described the cost as "enormous." "You don't know what you're doing (when you give it away). You can't know, and you certainly don't say, 'Everybody know me! Take away my privacy!'" He said, "And when it's gone, there's no underestimating how painful, strange and irrevocable that is. No matter how much you think I've enriched your life by being on the *X-Files*, if I had to do it again, I would seriously reconsider my choice."

Then there's the really unflattering aspect of my business, the part that's known to dine on people's insecurities and humanity - the ugly face of gossip and hearsay in its most destructive form. Even though I'm not a part of that kind of media, it's still very much a part of my business, and believe me the line between my kind of journalism and theirs is getting more unclear every day. I think back on the day *The New York Times* cited the *National Enquirer* as the source in the Clinton/ Lewinsky scandal ... and that's the day, in my opinion, all hell broke loose in the jungle.

The tabloids are nothing new. Celebrity watchers have been buying into them for years with the unspoken rule that they're gossip rags and the stories are made up ... but on that day I think everything changed and the lines went forever fuzzy.

So there I was, sitting on the proverbial fence. And then, as fate would have it my ending came to me, literally. She sauntered up to my microphone and sheepishly announced that doing press robs her of her soul. *"Really?"* I said, tell me more!

I first interviewed this gorgeous young actress years before, shortly after she arrived in Hollywood. At the time, she was totally naïve and about as green and wet behind the ears as they come. She even asked me why I was taking the time to interview her. "I'm nobody," she insisted. Since that afternoon in Burbank, she went on star in a successful TV series and several high profile movies. Yes, she was a *media virgin*, but she was also a talented, charming and funny young woman who was - and still is - earnestly building a career for herself.

Anyway, I'm doing the interview and I'm thinking about *Interview Tactics*, and writing something like, "Gee, the media is great, although far from perfect ..." when out of the blue, she makes her great confession. I felt it was almost as if she sought me out because she knew I needed this ending for the book. "Robs me of my soul," I pondered. Hmm ... I need to hear her story.

This is a woman who's smart, beautiful and talented with something to sell that's real and valuable, and she's also living proof of how interviews can go terribly wrong if you don't know how to handle the press. Because without *Interview Tactics,* the press can, and sometimes will, overstep their boundaries leaving you totally clobbered.

www.GaylMurphy.com

While she was telling me about her less than stellar experiences with the press, she also admitted how unprepared she still feels for the onslaught, and how she contantly wrestles with "that side" of the media you can only see when you're in the middle of it.

This is our unedited conversation and how I jumped off the fence ...

"(For the most part) I'm pretty happy now, I've grown up into not caring as much, but I have to tell you ... doing press robs me of my soul. Not questions like this because these are pretty rational; you know, not such dishy questions. I always want to do a good job with interviews even if they're not playing fair. I'm trying to do a good job and give them something of what they want, but still remain intact and not step on other people's toes trying to give someone a story or make myself look foolish. And that has killed me. I mean, I wake up in the middle of the night (thinking about it). The Foreign Press can be brutal because they're really writing for tabloids and stories that I don't take much stock in."

"Can't you just say, 'I don't want to answer that?'"

"Well you'd think so, but you can't with some people that aren't playing fair. Sure, you can say it and that gives them more reason to want to go in and see why it bothers you. 'Why aren't you answering it?' If you can act, if you can put on a face, I've found you can say, 'Oh you nosey little poop head. Yeah, sure, OK. Here's a little something.' And you give them something, even though you really don't want to. I'm sure there's people much more experienced than me. That's why it gets me down because I don't know how to navigate being polite, yet being firm. You know what boundaries I can have without pushing someone to dig deeper into something that's no one's business."

"It's not like you're one of those actresses who's in the headlines every week with a different guy, and even if you were ... what kinds of things do they pick on you for?"

"There's not really much in my life that I find that interesting for dish, and I don't even want to give them that much credibility by repeating them, but everyone's gonna find their thing. I'm a small girl, people dare to go to the 'thin issue,' which is so uninteresting to me. And it's just as weird as if I were 60 pounds heavier and I sat down, they wouldn't say, 'Well, you've put on the pounds, don't you think that's unhealthy? Don't you think you're setting a bad example for girls?' And I get a lot of that. 'Wow, you've really bought into the Hollywood thing, you're thin.' This is my body type. Just because I don't eat eight cupcakes a day anymore, I mean, I'm completely healthy with my life right now and I find it really upsetting when people really wanna make you feel unhealthy and you start to buy into it. Like, 'Oh God, should I cover up?' And I do it now because it's not worth questions to me. But that is upsetting (because) I take such good care of myself and now I feel for all the women … it's just strange."

"Do you think they look for things?"

"Of course they look for things. No one really cares about the color scheme of a movie when you're interviewing. Most people don't, unless you're doing NPR (National Public Radio) and there's some film-philes in there who really care about something technical or someone's vision. But for the most part, magazines sell dish. They sell fashion and weight issues and hair color and who's sleeping with whom. It's really upsetting to me. I get how it works and I've read some of them before, but it steals my soul and it makes me wonder, 'How can I get through this business?'"

"Have you stopped reading the print articles?"

"Yes, I don't read the print stuff anymore. Oh I'll pick it up if it's in the trailer, you know we all sit around … we have our magazines, I read them. But I've had a flawed life. I mean … I'm a woman. I'm not a child that's grown up in this business who's watched every step or had people watching my life. I've made mistakes, and they'll be out there. I just have to remind myself

that the people that love me will stand by me … end of story. But that's easier said than done. Sometimes you feel everyone's getting in your business. You know I'm here to just try and tell a story and entertain people and get my makeup done (laugh)."

"Doesn't all this make you think twice, like maybe I shouldn't be doing this?"

"Yeah, well then you're letting people that don't even know you or care about you take away something that you really enjoy. I'm sure if you're a really smart protective person, you learn how to do it in a way that can work for you without becoming a distant cold thing that's inaccessible to people. You know I'm not that savvy yet and a lot of actresses aren't. I'm not the only one and I'm not beating up on myself. I mean it's hard when you're in a situation where people ask you a question that's inappropriate. Sometimes it's hard just one-on-one to say, 'You're being inappropriate.' To a friend it's hard (to say) sometimes, not to mention thinking, 'How I answer this is gonna be judged by millions of people who might read or see this.' How do you answer that? I'm not saying this is impossible or the worst thing in my life. I'm just a regular girl from Michigan, you know, I tease people … I'm a regular mess-up sometimes, like a lot of people. And I (do an interview and) wake up at three o'clock in the morning saying, breathing heavily, 'Did I say anything that made that person sound like a bad person?' They'll interview me about friends or other actresses and you're wanting to sound candid and not guarded because that doesn't give the best impression of the person you're trying to speak of. It just gets into a whole thing and they're manipulative. It's not your average person having a conversation."

"Can you see it coming now?"

"I'm getting there, but I give people the benefit of the doubt and I believe there's good in everyone. Sometimes, there's just not any good in someone at any moment."

"So it's a balance then?"

"Yes, I think it's a balance. You figure out a way to make yourself comfortable and live with whatever is being asked of you. Just protect yourself and do what's right, I guess. And, I've yet to really learn it."

And that my friends is what I commonly refer to as A Road Kill Clobbering. And unfortunately, being torn apart by the media in this fashion occurs more times than you'd think. But the truth is, it doesn't have to happen ever, and especially to you because you've got survival skills now. And you've got 'em right here in your hot little hands. So I hope you'll take *Interview Tactics* to your heart, your head, your *zone* and your next interview and get out there tell your story like the media superstar you are!

INTERVIEW TACTICS

Celebrity Photo Gallery

"Murphy On The Move!"

Gayl Murphy - On the air holding down the fort at ABC's "Global Media Village" at the 2000 Academy Awards in Los Angeles, CA.

Jay Leno - Taken backstage at the NBC Studios in Burbank, CA. Jay was celebrating the *Tonight Show*'s first HDTV broadcast. Jay was his usual cordial, funny self!

Morgan Freeman - Always the consummate gentleman and one of my favorite movie stars. This was taken during the press interviews for *Kiss The Girls* in 1997. He signed it two years later.

The estimable Rudy Giuliani - At the Ritz Carlton Hotel in Pasadena, CA, during the HBO sessions of *Television Critics Association* Press tour, January 2002. Photo by my longtime friend Jonathan Exley.

Cameron Crowe - I am crazy for this guy, I admire him so much ... and he's a former neighbor! Snapped at the BFCA Awards Luncheon at the Beverly Hills Hotel in January 2000. Cameron won Best Screenplay for *Almost Famous*.

Michael Palin - Me and a Python! How many people can say that? Snapped in Pasadena, CA, 1999.

Russell Crowe - Also taken at the BFCA Awards Luncheon in January 2000. Russell won *Best Actor* award for his astonishing performance in *The Insider*. He should have also taken the Oscar.

Petty - When Tom Petty and the Heartbreakers and Bob Dylan announced they were going on the road together back in 1987, I showed up with my ABC/KLOS microphone in hand. This was an amazing double-bill tour. I saw the show twice, in Tacoma, WA, and Inglewood, CA.

David Bowie and Iman - This was taken on the red carpet at the Chinese Theater on Hollywood Boulevard at the premier of Mick Jagger's movie, *Freejack* in 1992. The producers of the film hired me to do the red carpet interviews … it was way too exciting.

Ann Wilson of Heart - One half of the *"rockin'est sister acts"* in rock 'n' roll. I interviewed Ann and Nancy on the road once in Roanoke, WV. We stayed up all night watching *The Woman* and yelling "Jungle Red!" at the screen. Photo taken in NYC, 1995.

John Corbett - Sorry John, but you'll forever be "Aiden" to me. Taken in March 2002 in Beverly Hills, CA, during the press interviews for *My Big, Fat Greek Wedding*. (We were singing the BBC song from *Austin Powers*.)

Woody Harrelson - What I remember most about this photo was how nice Woody was and that he gave me a great interview.

Tom Cruise - Taken in 1986 at the Westwood Marquis Hotel in Los Angeles, CA. Tom only did two radio interviews for *The Color Of Money*, and we had so much fun. He got a big laugh out of this photo when he signed it in December of 2001. He couldn't believe our hairdos either.

Johnny Depp - Taken at the press junket for *Don Juan De Marco* at the Four Seasons Hotel in Beverly Hills in 1995. Johnny signed the photo in 2001. What a cool guy.

Elton John - This photo was taken in the early 1990s at an Elton John/ Billy Jean King Charity Tennis event in Atlanta, GA. I was hired to do the TV and radio interviews for the event and, as always, EJ was a hoot.

Klaus Meine and Herman Rarebell of The Scorpions - The years I spent covering music afforded me access to some of my favorite rock bands, including these guys. Taken at their record company in the late 1980s.

Bono - This is one of my most cherished photographs. It was taken at a U2 press conference in Los Angeles, CA, in 1988 which eventually made it into their movie, *Rattle and Hum*. And the best part is, I also made it into the documentary!

I covered every U2 show in Southern California from 1982 to 1995 and wept each time.

Jimmy Page - This was taken at the *Guitar Center* in Hollywood, CA, the day Jimmy was inducted into *Rockwalk*. You'll have to go there yourself and read the sidewalk for the date. I'd never met Page one-on-one before that interview. He really surprised me. He was articulate, soft-spoken and really nice guy.

Van Halen - I've covered a million Van Halen shows in my career and this one was taken backstage at the first show of the *Monsters of Rock* tour in Wisconsin, 1989. I'll forever be a huge Van Halen fan.

Ted Nugent - This is one of my first photos as a reporter. It was taken in Ted's tour bus, parked outside the venue in Pasadena, CA, in 1982. Talking to him is like testifying in front of Congress ... only more fun.

Bill Maher - Taken at ABC's *Global Media Village* prior to the *Oscars* in 2002.

Emilio Estevez and Paula Abdul - When love was new and these two were the sweetest couple in Hollywood. Also taken on the red carpet at the *Freejack* premier in Hollywood, 1992.

John Mahoney - He might be grumpy on *Frasier*, but in front of my microphone he was fantastic. Los Angeles, CA, 2000.

Jonathan Winters - This was taken on the Warner Brother's lot in Burbank, CA.

The project escapes me, but being around this comedy icon was one of the biggest honors of my career. He's a giant.

Carlos Santana - New York City, 1995 at Sony Records. It's an honor to interview a superstar who not only has so much to say, but is also genuinely grateful for his success.

Billy Jean King, "Queen of the Court!" - Taken at the *Elton John/Billy Jean King Charity Tennis Event* in Atlanta, GA.

Pink Floyd Blimp - When Pink Floyd announced they were touring in the 1990s, the band chose to say it with a press conference and a blimp. This was taken at the "blimp pad" in Pasadena, CA, in 1994. Afterwards, I flew in the blimp. Pretty cool, we even cruised my house ... I waved.

Mick Fleetwood - This is also a very early photo. Taken in 1982 at UCLA, backstage, at an event called *Rock and Run.* To this day, I still have no idea what that means.

CLOCKWISE FROM TOP

Ted Danson, Bill Cosby, Bruce Willis and Tom Selleck - These are four celebrities whose acting careers and commitment to social causes I truly admire. And even now when I run into them, they remember me and will talk into my microphone. These photos were taken in the 1980s.

Me and my '57 Chevy Low-Rider - My first publicity still in 1981. I was "The Traffic Tootsie on the LA Freeway of Life." Taken while I was working at KWST radio in Los Angeles, CA. This photo and feature articles appeared in both the *LA Times* and the *LA Herald Examiner* within a week of each other. The car belonged to Ringo Starr and was loaned to me by Barris Custom Cars.

THE HOLLYWOOD "TALK OF FAME"

THE HOLLYWOOD
"TALK OF FAME"

After watching thousands of chat shows, listening to your favorite celebs and infoshamans on the radio, reading countless magazine and newspaper interviews, have you ever wonder what those people have to say about surviving the media? And what the Stars themselves think about going one-on-one with the press?

For example, who likes to be interviewed and who doesn't? Who gets clobbered and who doesn't? Who thinks every interview they do is awful? Well, I wondered over the years and it's something I've thought about a lot, especially since I'm the one on the other end of the microphone. So I decided to go on a mission, and address these burning questions. Some of the responses I got even blew me away!

The following section took years to assemble, but after inhaling *Interview Tactics: How To Survive The Media Without Getting Clobbered. The Insider's Guide To Giving A Killer Interview* you should be able to read between the lines with lots of really great insight on how to **tell it to sell it!**

Think of *Interview Tactics* as your own personal deadly weapon/ safety net whose sole purpose is to keep you from being pulverized by the press. Remember, there is no other book in the media jungle like *Interview Tactics* and no other place where these priceless morsels come together in such a sweet and cute little package.

John Travolta ★ "My favorite interview was with Martin Amis. It's my favorite interview because he embraced me in a way that I felt that he "got" who I was. I was his movie star and he explained to me that he was so happy with my comeback because he felt that somehow it paralleled with his life and, in doing so, he allowed me to be my 'smarter self.'

www.InterviewTactics.com

"On television I'd say Charlie Rose is my favorite interview. Charlie Rose has this uncanny ability to allow anyone that's on there be the 'smarter self' they are. You're in this room, it's dark, there's a round table, the lights dim, it's only you and him and these cameras that suddenly disappear, you have no sense of them. And he's asking you really bright questions that are not to challenge your intelligence, but to support your intelligence. And wow, you become the most articulate, the most creative and insightful self you can be.

"(I would say) Take the time to be as articulate as you can be, and if you find a question that you feel is unsavory on some level, take your time and work it out. Use communication as a tool to hone it and get to a result that you are happy with. Because you can do that, you don't have to just dismiss (the question), you can actually work it out. There are some times in rare moments, where a journalist will shut down - and it's been very rare - and doesn't want to hear what you have to say, but most of them do want to hear what you have to say. So therefore, you have an opportunity to actually clear up something that they're concerned about. The art is to not get upset about what they've asked, you know. That's the art of it, I think.*"

Cameron Diaz ★ "I don't read all of my interviews. I've read a few on occasion ... but it's hard. Maybe someone got bits and parts of me, but I think it's pretty much impossible for anyone to understand someone within a two-hour period which is usually what you get for an interview. In two hours you really can't explain who you are and someone can't really grasp who you are. They can only sort of get a taste of it, and I think even the more time they spend with you it's probably even more confusing.

"Because people are complex (you) just have to learn to give what is essential for the interview for whatever it is you're being interviewed for. And just put out a good positive ... or whatever it is you're in the mood for that day."

Kelsey Grammer ★ "There have been a couple of interviews that (I've done that) I thought were really good, the ones with which I've been most impressed with were the ones that have actually been truest to what I remember what I had said. I've not gotten into the habit that some of my friends have of recording it as well. It is remarkable the number of times - and this tends to be the rule - that I feel that the reviewer or the interviewer has come in with a predetermined point of view. That then the exercise of the interview really just becomes to collect a couple of quotable things to reinforce that point of view.

"It has been refreshing the times when I've sensed that there was not a point of view and that what actually occurred in the interview was a 'get acquainted' event which I like. One was an interview for *Playboy* magazine years and years ago where I thought, 'Well, she asked those questions and she actually had wrote what I said.' It was really refreshing. And then I've done several of course where I was just horrified. I did one for (a man's fashion magazine) that just absolutely sent me over the top of the moon, in a bad way. Where I thought he had misquoted me, I mean seriously misquoted things and I thought that was kind of irresponsible of him."

Sting ★ "Some people do understand you, some don't. I meet a lot of journalists and I talk to a lot of journalists and sometimes it can be very superficial, but you know, I try not to treat it as such because it can be significant for you and for them."

Jeff Bridges ★ "In my younger years it was like going to a psychiatrist or something, I've since learned not to deal with (the media) in that fashion. My particular path is to not give too much away. I try and intrigue the audience and tease them a little bit and make it sound like, 'Oh, that might be intriguing.'"

Sean Penn ★ "I find that I'm much more able to talk about things (that I've done) when I directed a movie (rather than) when I've acted in it. I can tell you anything that I've ever said in an interview, as an actor talking about acting, is just 'top of the head' hogwash. You just don't know what to say."

Kevin Spacey ★ "(An enjoyable interview) depends on who you're talking to. It depends on the quality of the questions. It depends on whether you think the interviewer actually saw the movie. Sometimes I'm actually convinced that the people that I'm sitting opposite of didn't go to the screening. It's quite clear to me when the questions are so unspecific, that it's like, 'Oh you read the notes, but you didn't go to the screening.' So I think there's a responsibility on that side. Do your work."

Matthew McConaughey ★ "What's fun about interviews is that I find I make contracts with myself, and I'll sit there and I won't have a planned answer and I'll say something that made sense (to me). Now I've made a contract that I'll explore that. Something that came out, or something that I believe in. That's what's nice and fun about interviews sometimes. Then you go back and read it and you don't even remember it. 'Did I say that?' And then sometimes you say, 'That didn't really come across right.' And then you go, 'Oh that's nice.' I mean, you sit there and you meet somebody and they know my biography ... you know I have a dog named Hud. And, you're thinking, 'I don't know if you're married or if you have kids. I don't know your first name, last name ... I don't know anything'. Already in the conversation there's an inherent unbalance. In ten minutes how well do you get to know somebody?"

Jim Carrey ★ "I (personally) am not really tempted to talk about myself at all generally, to be honest. When I come to something like this, in the car I'm going, 'Why do I do this? Why do I do this?' I don't like to talk about myself over and over again. But I generally have a good time when I'm doing it, but ultimately I'm not crazy about hearing my own voice. Many times I've had interviews where I've learned things about myself. I've had many interviews where I came out of it going, 'That was fun ... that was cool.' And I've also had interviews where I've felt the person was out to hurt me from the get-go. Or, I went home and thought, 'Oh that question ... oh that question ... oh man' as I didn't recognize the intent. I've had many different experiences. I have a theory about all this, (and that is) we all want to be part of the club."

Catherine Zeta-Jones ★ "It's really hard to get across what people want to see (because) they want to see *you*. They want to get a slice of what you really are or who you really are. And that's really difficult when you have three minutes or five minutes and the stopwatch is going and you have to plug the movie that you are sitting here for. The hardest thing for me and Michael [Douglas] is how much more we have to talk about other than our wedding and our child - especially when we have a great piece of material to sell - and it's exhausting. But the hardest thing is the preconception that people have of you which is completely wrong. And you find yourself in those ten minutes defending yourself, which is pretty bizarre. But I just like to make people - especially in the television interviews - get a slice of who you are for real. Because who they see on the screen is always totally different."

Laura San Giacomo ★ "I don't think this is an experience that I look forward to, but somewhere in the middle it starts to get comfortable. I think that if you want to be understood, if that's one of the things about you ... if there's something that you want be accurate about, you try to accurately express what you feel and that's sometimes difficult for anyone to do. And then sometimes we just sound so ridiculous, don't we? When we are talking about what we do. I mean, it just sounds so simply and utterly ridiculous the importance we place on this acting thing. You know what I mean? In the bigger scheme of things we don't need to get so serious about it.

"Remember what you're saying because many, many people will hear and that's something to be careful about. Look, we all have moments that we're embarrassed about and to be careful that you're not going to say something that you're gonna feel belongs to you. That's a little gem that's going out into the world and you have to make sure that it's OK that the world gets that. I think that's why I think about things - not like what I want to say and what I don't want to say - but what really, accurately represents who I am and how I do feel about whatever you're asking me and what's private for my own memory. And for the privacy of all the other people involved too because it goes to the world. I mean, anybody can record this and not everything is for everybody."

Halle Berry ★ "The media has been in very many ways good to me, especially being a black woman. Have I had my moments when I feel like I was beaten up on unfairly? Absolutely, but you know, all in all, the media has been a friend of mine. I know that, and I believe that's come about because of being honest. And I really don't have very much to hide; you know I really don't. And in the last four years of my life, I've become the kind of person who realizes that what people think about me really doesn't matter so much any more.

"Early on in my career I might have given an answer where I thought, 'This will be the good thing to say.' But as I've grown, I'm not that person anymore. I'm becoming more comfortable with who I am, and I know who I am. And if my words are twisted and somebody views me in a way that's not true ... then, hey, it's life and I can't really invest too much energy worrying about that. It's more important that I know who I am and what I mean when I say things. And, if it's misconstrued, then that's par for the course, that's what happens."

Daryl Hannah ★ "I would be the worst person to give anyone advice (on how to do an interview) because I suck at it. I've never been comfortable with it and I've never been good at it, and I've probably lost a lot of jobs because I don't (do press) very often. Some studios won't even hire me because I have a reputation for not doing press. (It's because) I'm awkward; I think it's kind of awkward. I love taking on a character, living in the skin of another person, but I'm very uncomfortable talking about myself.

"I accidentally went on a talk show once, I didn't mean to, I was just there and then they dragged me out and they were like, 'So, what are you doing here Daryl?' I said, 'Press Junket.' I just tend to try and answer the question, I don't say, 'Well, I just love la, la, la.' So there you go. (My advice would be) don't answer the question, just tell a funny story. That's the best way to deal with press."

Candice Bergen ★ "I infinitely prefer hearing someone else talk and learning about them or what they do, then yammering on endlessly myself. I've been doing this for such a long time that after you've been doing it; it's just hard to find anything interesting to say. So basically, I just try to be honest about things and keep a zone of privacy.

"It's not my goal in life to be a better interview, that's your problem and I know what that's like. I think (what having been an interviewer has done for me is) that I really respect journalism when it's practiced well. I know how difficult it is to interview someone who's been a public figure a long time and to try and find one stone that hasn't been unturned. And finally, all the stones have been turned except the ones that they don't want turned over and they usually like to keep them that way. So it's a challenge and I've always had respect for journalists."

Ray Liotta ★ "Does the public ever get to see me? They do if I'm shopping at Gelson's or pumping my gas … this is obviously not me pumping gas, so you definitely put out different things. I think that there's a certain decorum that should be with this. I know there are some actors that would be sitting here and smoking away on a cigarette and drinking beer and what not, and showing the true selves of what they are, but I'm not sure who really wants to see that. I try to answer everything based on how I feel. I know what to stay away from and what could look bad in print. So, you get a sense of somebody … but I also think, how much could you learn about somebody in like what? Fifteen minutes? And what are you gonna learn in 15 minutes? You have a job to do, so I think it's important to get the movie out. I know you've got an article to write so

I've got to be somewhat quotable and a little bit pithy. And then you do your job and I do my job and the movie gets out and we get paid and go home and pump the gas again.

"There's a job to be done here. For example, with this movie *(A Rumor of Angels)* you could ask me what death means to me. Well am I gonna go into what death means to me in 15 minutes? Now if it were an in depth thing where you were writing an article, and some articles you spend a day with somebody, or two days or a week, that's a whole different thing. But in this kind of forum, there's only so much you can do in 15 minutes."

Cindy Crawford ★ "I personally, for the most part, don't have any problems doing interviews and especially if there's a mutual respect. I think the hardest times that it's ever been for me is if you're going through something really traumatic personally, and unfortunately your personal life gets played out in the media and then you have to talk about it, when maybe you're not even ready to talk about it. That part is hard, but when I come to something like this ... I know the gig, you know the gig, I don't want to make it like pulling teeth, that's just painful for everybody. I come, I'm open, I'm here to talk and I want it to be a pleasant exchange of energy as opposed to, 'Oh, I really don't want to talk about that.' And I see those people and I think, 'Why even do the interview?' It's like they're so miserable doing it and that's their deal or whatever, but for me I like people. And sometimes it's just nice to get the feedback. Sometimes you get asked some really thought provoking questions and it makes you think about your career or your image or whatever."

Tim Robbins ★ "I prefer round table (radio and print) interviews to the one-on-one (TV) interviews. They're unbearable and it's no one's fault. It's a no-win situation for them too, because they have ... what? Three or four minutes to ask five questions? And they tend to be the same five questions. So, they're getting an exclusive interview, but they're also getting the same answers that everyone else is getting. And at the end of forty of those, you are a robot. So no one wins. It's very difficult to find out who a person is in twenty minutes.

www.GaylMurphy.com

"I personally have always been protective of who I am in my personal life and I've tried to separate it from 'this' - which is the promotion and the movie or to publicize something that's about to happen. I don't have a problem, (since) they're two separate things, and as long as you know they're separate in your mind. You try to get into a situation that's productive and positive and not adversarial. It's not a big deal."

Lisa Kudrow ★ "I don't know if this will be accurate or not, but whether the interview that I read in the paper is great or horrible, doesn't have that much to do with who I was during the interview. You know, I say something in a certain way and it gets printed - even if you're writing exactly what I'm saying - sometimes the irony is lost, or things get misunderstood or your interpretation of it is different, so how you characterize the quote will be different. I don't know, it's just like anything else, everyone has their own perception of who they're dealing with and what they're saying, and how they're trying to come across and how they really are - if they really are being who they are. I mean, those are things I can't control."

Sandra Oh ★ "What do I like about the interview process? When people ask me interesting questions (it makes me) constantly redefine why I do what I do. And I don't mind doing press at all because every so often you meet really nice people. So I find the process is OK.

"For anyone who had to do this? (I'd say) speak as honestly as possible, otherwise you'll get sick with your own fakeness. I tell you, people try and fake it out all the time. If you at least don't try to talk to someone for real - at least every fifth person that you talk to - you'll go crazy. Because you'll be sick of your own fakeness (laugh). You'll be smiling and saying the same thing over and over again, and hopefully if someone asks you an intelligent question you can really answer them. There's no point in talking to people if you're not communicating with them."

Jack Nicholson ★ "I think part of it with me is, I don't really want to be 'got,' that's why I don't do television interviews. I think that the less you're sure about me the more you're likely to get into a character I play. For me, to be really well defined in some super structural way would work against what I do. So it's high-folutin', but it's sort of what I think I'm about in that area. You know, I'm Irish ... I love to talk.

"If I'm on a roll, I think I can be pretty interesting on any one of a number of subjects, so who wouldn't like to be applauded for this? It's tempting, but I don't agree with it, so I don't do it. Television. Once you're on film (or video), there's no more room for interpretation. There you sit, however it's done. (Part of the reason I don't do television is) not wanting to be known. I've done a lot of print interviews and so forth with a lot of people who are - they're making a living, (and) I always assume they're talented at what they do. I make no mistakes about that. I'd say collectively, if you took those interviews and put them together, I'm in there somewhere."

James Woods ★ "Pretend you're in a deposition, and know that they'll ask you 95% of the questions and not care about the answer. They'll just wait till you're tired and wait to set up to destroy your reputation ... and I'm totally serious. I mean, you seem to be very nice, but sooner or later there's always somebody that decides they're gonna make a living chewing on your bones. So the press is unequivocally the enemy and just be as nice to them as you can but, you know, wait for the other shoe to drop because it will. **"**

Then doing interviews and meeting press isn't something you enjoy?

"Well, I enjoy it because you're being so nice. I mean, you're making a process I would not ever do again in my life - not for one second ever - if I didn't feel an ethical obligation to the film."

Billy Crystal ★ "You need to get the word out that you're in this movie and that you like it and it's good. And (for me) it's a requirement to my work and I feel like it's important for me to do. I've always been comfortable doing interviews, except when the movie's not that good."

John Lithgow ★ "It's interesting you should ask me (about junkets) because it is an interesting subject. I can sit at a junket like this; I mean, in these three days I'll probably speak to about 60 or 80 different journalists. They will ask almost all the same questions. With some of them I feel completely relaxed because they're funny, articulate and I will think of new angles, new thoughts, new takes on these questions. With others I just wilt in their presence. And I find it fascinating ... it's like a chemical.

"Sometimes I've made great friends with journalists. I treat (this process) as just meeting interesting people because journalists tend to be interesting people. Just because they're asking about me doesn't mean that they're not interesting. But like anything else, some people you meet and you immediately hit it off with and some people you know there's no future there."

Robert Downey Jr. ★ "There are certain boundaries, some stuff I don't want to talk about and it's pretty obvious when it comes up. If you don't have anything nice to say, don't say anything, and usually I'll do that ... but sometimes, I'll just say, 'Yeah, he was an (expletive).'"

Drew Barrymore ★ "I would say just be honest, you know ... the truth does set you free. And it's scary I think (but) when you're yourself it's just so much easier. You don't have to hide behind something or keep an act up, it's much more relaxed. And to enjoy it and have fun with it and realize how incredibly fortunate we all are. It's you that has the choice about how much you can enjoy your day or your life. You can kick through the day and be miserable and have to just get through it and complain, or you can thank God for each breath and make fun of it and put the joy in it and make it celebratory. It's really up to you."

Joey Fatone (*NSYNC) ★ "Just be yourself and answer the questions to the best of your knowledge. I mean, you can never really get prepped for this. You hear stories where people have gone through media classes or something to prep themselves, but for us, we got thrown into it. We didn't know any better. And I think that's a good thing because we'll tell you like it is. I'm here because I enjoy it and people need to know, obviously about what we're doing. And if people didn't want to know, I wouldn't be here."

Arnold Schwarzenegger ★ "This is radio, right? So here we have to talk in kind of complete sentences. Is that the idea? And repeat your question. Should I do that too?"

Have you been doing some kind of media training, or something lately?

"No, but that's what they always say, 'Can you repeat the question because I can not cut myself into this.' Or, 'How close (to the mikes) do you want me to get?'"

Are you comfortable giving interviews?

"I enjoy all kinds of interviews. I love it."

... especially radio, huh?

"Well, radio is a whole different ball game because you can really communicate with the people. I love radio interviews (tongue firmly implanted in his cheek). I'm dying to do radio interviews. I always wish that all my interviews were radio interviews."

Lance Bass (*NSYNC) ★ "I'm very comfortable in front of media. I'm probably more comfortable in front of media than other things I do. I'm just so used to it. We've always gotten along with the media and I think we have this special connection that I don't think any other artist has just because we have fun with them and they have fun back. Of course they'll criticize because that's what they do, and we learn from that. I mean,

www.GaylMurphy.com

we read the reviews and we learn and we try to change it, and even recently it's been great - the kind of support we've gotten from everybody. So we have a really good situation."

Do you think any reporter ever got to you?

"I think so ... they definitely push as far as they can because that's what they do. I mean they want something to happen because we're so normal and we don't have any drama in our lives, that they want to find something, you know? They're trying to create stuff sometimes - and I think they give up a lot of times - but we're so open and everyone knows so much about us already that there's nothing to hide."

Kurt Russell ★ "I like people. You know we're in a business where we want people to have a good time at the show, so you should tell them about it. I don't have any beef with the press as far as when you're trying to get information out there to the people. My beef's in other areas."

Kevin Costner ★ "I've always been more of a worker bee type personality, even in my films. I can conduct myself on the Red Carpet, but I can tell you, it's not my favorite place to be. This (being interviewed) is not my favorite place to be."

Denzel Washington ★ "I hope I'm better (at being interviewed) than when I first started. I know I'm more relaxed. You know they pay us a lot of money (to do this) and this is a business, it's called Show Business. And a part of the business is selling the product you know, the film. And that's why I'm here. I mean, you're a nice person, but I'm here to sell the film. That's what I do. 'Celebrity', or being in the business long enough ... I now don't do this other than when I'm selling a movie. I don't need to be known. I don't consider myself a celebrity and don't really want to be one. I don't go to premieres and I don't do all that kind of stuff because it doesn't really have anything to do with really what I do, I'm an actor."

Dyan Cannon ★ (Is Hollywood forgiving?) "I think so. I'd like to think so. I think Hollywood has a big heart and I think

Hollywood is very forgiving, thank God". (Is that a good thing?) "You betchya. My Gosh there are things that happened to me years ago that several members of the press got a hold of and did nothing with and I'll love those people as long as I live, you know. 'Cuz they had enough love in their heart not to write about it and spare me stuff."

"I've had great experiences with the press and great experiences with Hollywood and I think that people in Hollywood know that you screw up and there's still room to straighten that screwup out." (And for the people who always complain that they're being followed everywhere?) "I kinda think they want to be followed or they wouldn't be going there."

Bruce Willis ★ "I don't know what the real appeal of 'celebrity' (is), I truly don't understand it. I don't know why that stuff is more important than politics or why people know more about actors than the guys who are spending their tax dollars."

Wesley Snipes ★ "How do you learn to deal with the loss of anonymity (and) the loss of privacy? You just pray."

Steve Martin ★ "The interview process is a little bit of a performance, it's a little bit defensive ... depending on your nature, and it can be redundant. But also, it's also fun to talk about yourself and have everybody stare like they're really interested. And every once in awhile it comes along and you kinda learn how to do it, and hopefully have fun doing it."

Matt Damon ★ (How much do I keep for myself and how much do I give away?) "Well, that is actually a really good question and it's not something I think I know, I think it's something I'm trying to figure out. Because I have friends who do it to varying degrees. I mean, Edward Norton does very little press and I've talked to him a lot about it and he's got a really good point about it. Just as an actor, he can play a wider range of characters because people don't have any preconceived notions about him. And the less people know about you, the more leeway you have as an actor to play a wider range of roles. So I understand that theory. But, there's also the reality that you want people to see your movie, you know? And so it's hard to find the balance of well, I want to promote the movie, I'm proud of the movie and the work everybody did, but I want to maintain enough privacy that I don't feel raped by it. So I guess the long-winded answer is that I'm still working on it. But, it's not the worst thing in the world, people whine about it a lot. It's not like pulling teeth. This beats a root canal."

Geena Davis - (When I'm answering questions) "It's just what feels right. I definitely can tell when it's something I don't want to talk about. And then I can either dance around it and maybe you don't even notice, or I can say, 'I'd rather not answer that.'"

Robin Williams ★ (I'm comfortable doing this) "... because I like you. It's the opposite of Sally Field, (Putting on a voice) 'I like you, I really like you.' Seriously, I have fun. This is nothing scary, I mean there's nothing I have to hide except my fur. But you know that. And this is radio ... and I haven't had pants on the entire time. What do I do? I have fun. I love watching you guys trying not to laugh; it's so much fun. It's a blast; it doesn't scare me. We have good fun as we always do."

Goldie Hawn ★ (How has talking to the media changed for me over the years?) "Oh, that's a good question. I don't hang on to anything anymore (because) there's nothing to protect. But, I'm not sure I had much to protect in the early days either. I mean, I was pretty forthright about who I was. I wasn't much of a person who hides behind anything."

Michael Vartan ★ "I keep saying this, and it sounds like such a depressed way of living life, but it's actually really freeing ... I'm gonna be dead in fifty years and who cares? I try to be honest, I mean, you guys are doing your jobs and I can only assume being a reporter and talking to an actor (that has an attitude) ... I mean what's the point? Why even come here if I'm gonna act like. (Putting on a voice) 'Well, you know the movie ... I gotta say that the arcs are ... (blah, blah, blah).' That's a waste of time and if you're gonna do that, don't even do (the interview)."

Seth Green ★ (What do I think of junkets?) "Listen, I think we both know this is a mutual responsibility and we've got to respect each other and make it as fun as we can. It's your job and it's my job. So I don't mind it, it's exhausting, definitely. My throat gets sore by the end of two hundred interviews, and I really just try not to perform it by rote. So I let myself hear every question for the first time and I listen to what you have to say and I try to answer you as honestly as I'm willing to do."

Carson Daly ★ "I know you're looking for soundbites (here) so I'll try and make my sentences complete, and I'll pause for the edit … just kidding. We had Conan O'Brian do one of our test shows and he was the best guest in the world because he does Late Night. So I'd ask, in his case, early on - probably a really dumb question - and he would be gracious enough to give me a really good complete, solid answer with some tidbits in it and it made the show really good. So I try to be a good interview because I understand what it's like to have a crappy one."

Dick Clark ★ (In print) "You can't see a facial expression; you don't have a voice tone or anything. I look at your print contemporaries every now and then … I read one the other day from a guy where I said something to him in levity, 'Yeah you fool, you think so and so.' And, he printed it that way and it made me sound really mean and angry and I said it with a chuckle. And you can't translate that."

Jill Hennessey ★ "How do I know how much to give? To be honest, maybe I give too much because I don't censor myself. I have a very hard time trying to control things. I don't feel comfortable not being honest or expressing how I feel. And I just enjoy myself more if I'm just honest with everybody I'm dealing with. Whether it's my co-workers, cast members, producers, media, photographers … and I'm here to have a good time. You know, everybody's trying to do their job. You're doing me a favor by doing this interview, so what's the point in regimenting things?"

Matthew Lillard ★ (On Sarah Michelle Gellar) "I can answer this because I've watched her do international (press) and I've seen her do this over a hundred times. I give so much credit to her because the way she handles these scenarios is unbelievable. Internationally, the way they ask questions was very insulting to me. The fact that she can do it with grace and style and keeps her life to herself, and yet can sell a film, and dodge and weave and still come off smelling like a roses is unbelievable. That's why she's been around so long and will continue to be a star."

INTERVIEW TACTICS

"*The Workbook*"

How to Survive the Media Without Getting Clobbered!

"The Insider's Guide To Giving A Killer Interview!"

by Gayl Murphy,
Hollywood Correspondent

www.InterviewTactics.com

Interview Tactics

THE WORKBOOK ✍ PART ONE!

How DO I Prepare To Talk To The Media?

"It's hard to find the balance of well, I want to promote the movie ... but I want to maintain enough privacy." ★ Matt Damon

Ralph Waldo Emerson said, *"You are what you think about all day long."* And that is so true. It's also something to keep in mind while attempting to navigate your way through media-landscape. If you really want to give a killer interview, then I urge you to take the time and think about your life and decide how you want the rest of the world to perceive you. And how you want it to see your product, your company and your achievements.

This Is A Test of the Emergency Broadcast System! This Is Only A Test! ... OK, so it's not *really* a test, but it is an ... *Interview Workbook!*

"(People) want to get a slice of who you really are and that's difficult when you have three minutes or five minutes." ★ Catherine Zeta-Jones

We've now arrived at the audience participation portion of our journey through the media jungle: How to talk to the press and give them what they want! In other words, how to find *your* story. Remember, **"You gotta tell it to sell it!"**

www.InterviewTactics.com

It's about that time in your *Interview Tactics* training that we start using the *Interview Tactics Workbook!* Now, some of you might not wish to write directly in your book, and that's fine. So, consider getting a separate journal apart from this book, or you may receive the entire workbook free via eMail by sending a blank email to: Workbook@InterviewTactics.com.

You'll also need a really great pen and a yellow highlighter. If you choose to keep a separate book, think of that book as your *Interview Tactics Workbook.* What we're about to do here is uncover your story so we can connect it all together. But first, we have to *find* your story.

With your workbook in front of you and your pen in hand, ask yourself the following questions, and make sure you write complete answers. Let yourself and your mind go. See pictures and describe them. Don't censor yourself and *don't stop.* Just let your pen take you where it wants to go!

Be SPECIFIC! Give DETAILS!
Write PARAGRAPHS!

Read the questions in the workbook first so that you get a grasp on where I'm coming from, and then go back and answer the questions.

Helpful Hints for Answering the Interview Tactics Workbook Questions to Finding *Your Story* ...

You know how athletes talk about being in *the zone* when they're playing? Sort of like the scenes in the movie *For the Love of the Game,* when Kevin Costner steps onto the pitchers mound and uses the voice inside his head to "clear the system" so he can shut out the crowd and just be. The *zone* is that special place that all champions go to in their head. It's the quiet place inside where it's just them and the ball and the game, and where they want to go next. Kinda like a Yoda thing. Before we go any further, let's talk about your *personal zone* for a minute, because that's where I want you to be when you're writing in this workbook. I want you to hang out there in your head with your product, invention, songs, investment guide, videos, expert advise, formula, procedure, coaching system, script or whatever your product or service is, and answer every question as best you can.

And while you're in your *zone*, think along the lines: "If I were at a party, a convention, a networking group, a pitch meeting or *The Tonight Show* what is it about my life/job/profession/creation that people would find interesting?"

The goal of the *Interview Tactics Workbook* and this process is to get you connected, familiar, close and intimate with all the parts of you and your personality that contributed to the creation of your product or service. OK, now go back and answer the questions.

Take all the time you need. Days, weeks, months ... if that's what it takes. And keep in mind, this journal and workbook is an ongoing process, so don't expect to write a bunch of paragraphs in a weekend and that's it. This journey is constantly evolving, changing and growing, just like you.

And now for the **Interview Tactics Workbook** to finding ... YOUR STORY!

1. What *exactly* is it that you do?

_____

_____

_____

_____

_____

_____

_____

_____

_____

_____

_____

_____

_____

_____

_____

_____

_____

_____

_____

_____

_____

2. In a perfect world, how would you like people to perceive you and what you do?

3. What would you like the world to know about you and what you do?

_____

_____

_____

_____

_____

_____

_____

_____

_____

_____

_____

_____

_____

_____

_____

_____

4. When someone uses your product or service, reads your book or hears your music, what message do you want to send to the listener? What do you want them to hear? How do you want them to feel?

_____

_____

_____

_____

_____

_____

_____

_____

_____

_____

_____

_____

_____

_____

_____

_____

5. What's so unique about you or your movie, book, project, medical discovery, product or company?

6. What's the most interesting thing about it? *(Go there in your mind's eye and revisit that place. Be specific. Think color and detail.)*

_____

_____

_____

_____

_____

_____

_____

_____

_____

_____

_____

_____

_____

_____

_____

_____

7. Just how DID you get interested in what you're doing?
(Take a walk down memory lane and be as specific as you can.)

_____

_____

_____

_____

_____

_____

_____

_____

_____

_____

_____

_____

_____

_____

_____

Why would someone want to read or hear about you? *(Don't worry about being egocentric, this assignment is for your eyes only.)*

_____

_____

_____

_____

_____

_____

_____

_____

_____

_____

_____

_____

_____

_____

_____

_____

8. Would you want to read or hear about you? Why? *(Again, be as specific as you can.)*

_____

_____

_____

_____

_____

_____

_____

_____

_____

_____

_____

_____

_____

_____

_____

_____

_____

9. What is it that you've done that's so extraordinary?

_____

_____

_____

_____

_____

_____

_____

_____

_____

_____

_____

_____

_____

_____

_____

_____

_____

_____

10. Just how colorful, dangerous or emotional was the rocky road to success? Now's your chance to really sell it. *(And here's a clue, choose one thing and elaborate on it.)*

_____

_____

_____

_____

_____

_____

_____

_____

_____

_____

_____

_____

_____

_____

_____

_____

_____

_____

_____

_____

_____

_____

_____

_____

_____

_____

_____

_____

_____

_____

_____

_____

_____

_____

INTERVIEW TACTICS
WORKBOOK ✍ PART TWO!
Write Down Your "Talking Points"

Now, with your pen and highlighter, go back over your answers to the *Interview Tactics Workbook: Part One* and bullet-point every important and colorful item of each and every answer.

Then highlight all those bite size pieces of your story and set them aside to "breathe" for awhile.

As you're going over your workbook answers, be ruthless, edit like crazy and be as specific as you possibly can. You should have lots and lots of information to work with now.

By jumping into this editing process, you're creating several shorter and more detailed stories of all the different facets of your product, service, life and persona - all in one body ... yours. Remember what we talked about earlier: we live in a soundbite culture; people love *meaty, media morsels!* These golden highlights of story are what I call your *talking points*, and this is where it gets good.

This section is designed for you to write down your *talking points*. Don't worry about sentence structure or punctuation. Your focus here is to get those *golden nuggets* of your story out there so you can see them!

_____

_____

_____

_____

_____

_____

_____

_____

_____

_____

_____

_____

_____

_____

_____

_____

_____

_____

_____

_____

_____

_____

_____

_____

_____

INTERVIEW TACTICS
WORKBOOK ✍ PART THREE!
Soundbites That Grab Me!

So, you think you know what a soundbite looks and sounds like now? Try writing some down, and be sure to reread them after you're done! (See page 44 for more details.)

_____

_____

_____

_____

_____

_____

_____

_____

_____

_____

_____

_____

_____

_____

_____

_____

_____

_____

_____

_____

_____

_____

_____

_____

_____

_____

_____

_____

_____

_____

_____

_____

_____

_____

_____

INTERVIEW TACTICS
WORKBOOK ✎ PART FOUR!
Combine Your Talking Points
With Your Soundbites!

Now that you've completed your *talking points*, and you're familiar with what soundbites are, use this page to create some soundbites of your own! Create at least three different versions: a five-second grabber, a 15-second and a 30-second ... and have fun!

_____

_____

_____

_____

_____

_____

_____

_____

_____

_____

_____

_____

_____

_____

_____

_____

_____

_____

_____

_____

_____

_____

_____

_____

_____

_____

_____

_____

_____

_____

_____

_____

_____

_____

MEET THE AUTHOR

Gayl Murphy, Hollywood Correspondent

The *Los Angeles Times* wrote at length about Hollywood correspondent Gayl Murphy both times she traveled to the People's Republic of China to report the state of pop music there. The *Times* affectionately characterized her as the "Peripatetic entertainment reporter" that she is, and then chronicled her again when she "Happily went to 'The Wall' for Rock 'n' Roll in Berlin," after filing a series of news features on the emerging music scene in a newly reunified Germany.

In addition to assignments in Beijing, Shanghai and Berlin, Murphy's travels in broadcasting have taken her throughout Europe, Canada, Mexico, Japan and the Caribbean. In her on-air career, which spans over two decades, Murphy estimates she's interviewed more than 10,000 celebrities.

Affiliated with the BBC in Los Angeles, Murphy's commentaries and celebrity interviews have appeared on television, radio and in print worldwide. As a Hollywood TV Correspondent on for E! Television's *The Gossip Show* and the BBC's *Liquid News*, she also "tells it like it is" in her column *Spotlight On Hollywood* for *Ultimate DVD* magazine. Murphy has also covered Hollywood for a number of entertainment-based websites, including MrShowBiz, AOL's Entertainment Asylum, and WallOfSound - and consults *Sirius Satellite Radio* and *The Celebrity Edge.*

Over the years, her fine-tuned reporting skills have been sought after by media organizations worldwide. Always one to track a great story, Murphy's interviews and news features have appeared on ABC News, ABC Radio Networks, ABC Radio International, ABC Television, BBC Radio, BBC Television, MCM Networking/Australia, MCM Networking/ Europe, KFI/LA, *US Magazine*, Artists Services/Australia, WENN/UK, *NOW Magazine*/Australia, SFX Radio, Winstar Radio, KFWB/LA, Canadian Broadcast Company, XRadionet, *Film Review Magazine*, *ROCK Magazine*, AP Radio, Global Satellite Network and Sony Worldwide Radio Networks.

Murphy's humble beginnings in broadcasting sprang to life in "The City of Angels," after wrangling her way on to the airwaves at KROQ as the voice of the lovely and talented German dominatrix Greta La Gumbo on *The Young Marquis Show.* Upon abdicating her black leather corset, she jumped the dial to KWST and created the affable, and always timely *Traffic Tootsie* - complete with a '57 Chevy and spongy dice!

Leaving her low rider behind, Murphy moved on to KLOS and ABC News for the next 17 years. It was at KLOS that she reinvented herself yet again as Los Angeles' first and only, *Backstage Entertainment and Concert Reporter* - regularly broadcasting live from huge rock concerts and entertainment events throughout the world. For the ABC News she reported on Hollywood, celebrities, films, television and popular culture.

It's Murphy's 'take no prisoners' broadcasting persona that motivated *The Hollywood Reporter* to acknowledge her for being the "Media Veteran" she is, and *Performance Magazine* to sum her up as "Mainstay Gayl Murphy, one of this town's only on-air reporters covering the Hollywood scene!"

For her contributions in public service broadcasting, Murphy is the recipient of a SUNNY Award from the Southern California Broadcasters Association, two Certificates of Merit Awards from the County of Los Angeles and two Finalist Awards from the International Radio Festival of New York.

Murphy is a member in good standing of The Broadcast Film Critics Association, American Federation of Television and Radio Artists and The Screen Actors Guild.

For more information about Gayl Murphy, her seminars, INTERVIEW TACTICS workshops and other products, please contact the author:

GAYL MURPHY PRODUCTIONS, INC.
Gayl Murphy, Hollywood Correspondent
1300 North Cahuenga Boulevard, Suite 118
Hollywood, California 90038 USA

Internet ✆ www.GaylMurphy.com
eMail ✉ Gayl@GaylMurphy.com

Internet ✆ www.InterviewTactics.com
eMail ✉ Gayl@InterviewTactics.com

INTERVIEW TACTICS!

How To Survive The Media
Without Getting Clobbered!

with GAYL MURPHY,
Hollywood Correspondent

Hollywood Entertainment Reporter, Gayl Murphy, is accepting new clients for private one-on-one, corporate and workshop interview training. Including interview coaching, media consulting and interview skills training!

**Gayl Murphy says, *"You gotta TELL IT to SELL IT!
If you can't TELL IT - You can't SELL IT!"***

To schedule an appointment, contact Gayl Murphy:

GAYL MURPHY PRODUCTIONS
Gayl Murphy, Hollywood Correspondent
Internet ⌐ www.GaylMurphy.com
eMail ✉ Gayl@GaylMurphy.com

Fees vary according to the length of the presentation, size of the workshop and the degree of customization required.

Interview Tactics Coaching Success Story:

"Gayl Murphy gave our professional team several new tools for approaching the media. They learned to anticipate questions and refine their message. They discovered how to expand an interview to make a key point. Participants also practiced in front of a live video camera with a seasoned interviewer — an experience that one researcher called 'illuminating.' Interview Tactics helped enhance the skills necessary for effective print, radio and TV interviews." ✧ John L. Colonghi, Vice President of External Affairs, Buck Institute for Age Research, Novato, California

INTERVIEW TACTICS!

How To Survive The Media Without Getting Clobbered!

with GAYL MURPHY, Hollywood Correspondent

With the explosion in media, it seems like everyone is being booked for interviews these days! TV, radio, print, you name it ... So, what about you? Will you be ready to step up to the microphone when your big break comes? Do you have what it takes to "talk to the camera" about your latest movie, CD, script, product, service, business or accomplishment? If you're gonna sell it, you've gotta be able to tell it. And if you can't tell your own story, who will?

INTERVIEW TACTICS IS THE INSIDER'S GUIDE TO GIVING A KILLER INTERVIEW!

This lively media training will prepare you to go one-on-one with the press, give killer interviews and not get clobbered in the process. And it will include actual soundbites from celebrity interviews - the good, the bad and the unable.

Veteran correspondent, Gayl Murphy has done over 10,000 celebrity interviews in her on-air career - and she knows better than anyone *"you've got to tell it to sell it,"* and that being interviewed is a give and take process. Murphy will teach you what to give and what to take:

◆ **What are the RULES!**
◆ **How to master the art of meeting the press!**
◆ **How to talk to a reporter!**
◆ **What reporters want from you so you can give it to 'em!**
◆ **The different kinds of media and what they look for!**
◆ **What a soundbites is and how to talk in soundbites!**

- ◆ **How to get to the point when you speak!**
- ◆ **Press tours, roundtables and the Red Carpet!**
- ◆ **On and off the record!**
- ◆ **How to find and package your story!**
- **... and much, much more!**

For upcoming INTERVIEW TACTICS seminar dates and times, please go to: www.InterviewTactics.com

Seminar & Workshop Success Stories:

"Gayl's course is a must for anyone interested in any sort of public life or needs publicity for their project. Her seminar gives you the tools you need to stand out while not being overbearing. You will learn how the media thinks, how to work with them, and what they need to help you to successfully promote your project or skill. I can directly equate hundreds of successful interviews to Gayl's teachings!" Dr. Dennis W. Neder, Author of Being a Man in a Won◇in's World

"Gayl Murphy's IT seminar gave me the ground rules I needed so I could 'tell it to sell it'. I learned how to 'tell my story' while being concise and factual. A reporter wants to do a good job too, so 'don't be afraid, have fun and be energetic.' I learned a lot of valuable interviewing skills and I've used what I've learned in my music publishing business." Allison Caine of Lou Handman Music ✧

"Gayl, thanks for your outstanding class! I was there to learn how to give better interviews and what I learned is that when you interview, you give your subject your undivided attention. No acting about it. You appeared totally interested, thoughtful and concerned like you were in the zone" Karen Little (New York), www.LittleViews.com ✧

Gayl Murphy's reports on film, TV, music and popular culture have appeared on BBC Television, BBC Radio, ABC News, ABC Radio Networks, E! and online at ABCNews.com and MrShowBiz.com.

GAYL MURPHY'S WEB SITE

www.GaylMurphy.com

Hollywood Correspondent
& Interview Expert

MEET GAYL MURPHY!

Hollywood Entertainment Reporter! Covering Films, Television, Music and Popular Culture!

"Median Veteran" ... *The Hollywood Reporter*
"Peripatetic Entertainment Reporter" ... *L.A. Times*

Hollywood Correspondent, **Gayl Murphy**, offers an insider's look at some of the **celebrities**, **star-studded events**, and **movers and shakers** she's reported on, worked with and interviewed in Hollywood!

There are also lots **tinsel town treasures** too: **photos**, **backstage passes** and other **goodies** to peruse ...

SOUNDBITES - Click and hear what your favorite stars are "dishing" about! **You don't want to miss this!**

GOODIES - Straight from Gayl Murphy's personal media archive, check out some of her classic rock 'n' roll memorabilia and "way cool" photographs!

FEATURES - Selected news stories, feature articles and full-length interviews. You can also read Gayl's column - **SPOTLIGHT ON HOLLYWOOD** - featured monthly in *Ultimate DVD Magazine*.

In addition to reporting on **Hollywood** and the **entertainment industry**, Gayl has developed a very exciting and unique **Interview** and **Media Skills Training** that she's been teaching - with great success - in New York, Los Angeles, San Francisco and San Diego. And you can learn more about it!

SEMINARS - In a group setting, Gayl will teach you how to fine tune your interview skills and prepare for the media the first time or the next time you step up to the microphone.

COACHING - Gayl will teach you one-on-one exactly what you need to know to develop or jump-start your interview skills, and how to perfect your unique story! Remember, *you gotta to tell it to sell it!*

CONTACT INFO - If you wish to contact Gayl Murphy, you may do so either on the web or via eMail:

GAYL MURPHY PRODUCTIONS, INC.
Gayl Murphy, Hollywood Correspondent
1300 North Cahuenga Boulevard, Suite 118
Hollywood, California 90038 USA

Internet 🖰 www.GaylMurphy.com
eMail ✉ Gayl@GaylMurphy.com

Internet 🖰 www.InterviewTactics.com
eMail ✉ Gayl@InterviewTactics.com

PRESS KIT INFORMATION - Looking for press release information about Gayl Murphy and her NEW BOOK, *Interview Tactics*? Look no further!

- ☑ Press Release Information
- ☑ Gayl Murphy Personal Profile and Biography
- ☑ Press Clippings & More

PARTNER LINKS & AFFILIATES

- ☑ Entertainment/Talent Industry Partners
- ☑ Internet Marketing, eBook & Self-Publishing, Radio Publicity & Other Marketing Resources
- ☑ E-Commerce, Shopping Carts & Merchant Accounts
- ☑ Book Printing Services For The Self-Publisher
- ☑ CD/CD-ROM & DVD Duplication Services
- ☑ Personal & Professional Self-Improvement

www.GaylMurphy.com
Hollywood Correspondent
& Interview Expert

INTERVIEW TACTICS PARTNERS & ASSOCIATE RESOURCES

ENTERTAINMENT/TALENT INDUSTRY PARTNERS

◆ **JEFF KRAVITZ ...** Jeff Kravitz is a celebrity photographer among other talents. Jeff's clients include MTV, HBO, Dreamworks, Miramax, *Rolling Stone* and *US Magazine*. Visit www.FilmMagic.com ...

◆ **DEAN HENDLER ...** Dean Hendler is a Los Angeles based production still photographer for film, television, commercials and music. Visit www.DeanHendler.com ...

◆ **JONATHAN EXLEY ...** Jonathan specializes in portraits of celebrities, sports figures, politicians, fashion beauties, authors and many more. Visit www.ExleyPhoto.com ...

INTERNET MARKETING, EBOOK & SELF-PUBLISHING, RADIO PUBLICITY & OTHER MARKETING RESOURCES

◆ **SELF-PUBLISHING & TOTAL MARKETING TACTICS ...** Bart Smith, TheMarketingMan.com, author of TOTAL MARKETING TACTICS, has written one of the most affordable and condensed Internet marketing and self-publishing "HOW-TO" books available via CD-ROM/eBook on the Internet today!

TOTAL MARKETING TACTICS is jam-packed with over 2,700 stealth-like marketing tactics, web site links, resources, organized and categorized simply to help promote, market and expose your business, web site, book, eBook, service, seminar and/or product in a tactical, efficient and orderly manner.

TOTAL MARKETING TACTICS is laid out in well-organized categories such as eBook Marketing Tactics, Search Engine Submission Tactics, eZine Marketing Tactics, Affiliate Marketing Tactics, Self-Publishing and Author Marketing Tactics, Daily/Weekly "Do-This" Checklists, Press Release Marketing Tactics, Copyright & Protection Information and so much more! An all-in-one resource like you've never seen! Guaranteed to blow your "marketing brain" away! Visit www.TheMarketingMan.com ...

◆ **MARKETING WITH POSTCARDS** ... Alex Mandossian, acknowledged as the top expert in the field of postcard marketing, says the most overlooked marketing secret is the humble postcard. Postcards can dramatically increase sales and profits without spending an extra dime on advertising, marketing or promotional costs. Visit www.MarketingWithPostcards.com ...

◆ **FREE RADIO MARKETING & PUBLICITY** ... Alex Carroll, Radio Publicity Expert, can show you how to secure FREE radio publicity! Become rich and famous as a guest on big radio shows without ever spending a dime on advertising, or ever leaving the comfort of your very own home. Visit www.FreeRadioMarketing.com ...

◆ **SIMPLE MARKETING PRINCIPLES** ... Debbie Bermont is the President of Source Communications. Debbie's marketing philosophy can be summed up in two words: Simplicity & Action! Visit www.SimplePrinciples.com ...

INTERNET SHOPPING CARTS & E-COMMERCE

◆ **1SHOPPINGCART.COM** ... Fully integrated shopping cart and marketing system software including online database management, eMail broadcasting capabilities, autoresponders, ad tracking software, affiliate tracking software (and so much more) ... all rolled into one! Visit www.1ShoppingCart.com ...

BOOK PRINTING SERVICES FOR THE SELF-PUBLISHER

◆ **DeHART's PRINTING SERVICES** ... When it's time to print your next book, *DeHART's Printing* can print, deliver and fulfill your book order no matter how small the quantity! Get your next book, journal, catalog or other publication out faster with *DeHART's Printing*. Visit www.DeHarts.com ...

PERSONAL & PROFESSIONAL SELF-IMPROVEMENT

◆ **NLP TRAINING, SEMINARS, COACHING & PRODUCTS** ... Gary De Rodriguez, Master NLP Practitioner and Trainer for personal and professional for development. Your resource for NLP Books, Videos, Tapes, Group Seminars and Personal Coaching. Visit www.LifeDesignTraining.com ...

To Order More Copies of Interview Tactics!

Internet Orders: www.InterviewTactics.com

Fax Orders to: (323) 417-5172 (Credit Card Orders Only)

Regular Postal Mail Orders to:

GAYL MURPHY PRODUCTIONS
1300 North Cahuenga Boulevard, Suite 118
Hollywood, California 90038 USA

For postal orders, mail this order form with your payment to the above address. Do not send cash and no COD's. Thank you!

PLEASE SEND FREE INFORMATION ON:

❑ Seminars   ❑ Coaching   ❑ Mailing List   ❑ Other Products

Name:_____

Address:_____

_____

City:_____

State/ZIP:_____

Country:_____

Phone Number:_____

eMail Address:_____

Credit Card: ❑ Visa   ❑ Master Card   ❑ AMEX

Credit Card#:_____

Expiration Date:_____

Billing Address:_____

_____

City:_____

State/ZIP:_____

Country:_____

PRICE: $29.95 ($US) plus $5.00 ($US) S&H ... *Per Book!*

CA Residents Add 8.25% Sales Tax
International Orders Add $5.00 ($US) EXTRA Per Book

TOTAL $ _____ ENCLOSED!

Prices and availability subject to change without notice. Please allow one to three weeks for delivery. Thank you for your order!

To Order More Copies of Interview Tactics!

Internet Orders: www.InterviewTactics.com

Fax Orders to: (323) 417-5172 (Credit Card Orders Only)

Regular Postal Mail Orders to:

GAYL MURPHY PRODUCTIONS
1300 North Cahuenga Boulevard, Suite 118
Hollywood, California 90038 USA

For postal orders, mail this order form with your payment to the above address. Do not send cash and no COD's. Thank you!

PLEASE SEND FREE INFORMATION ON:

❑ Seminars ❑ Coaching ❑ Mailing List ❑ Other Products

Name:_____

Address:_____

_____

City:_____

State/ZIP:_____

Country:_____

Phone Number:_____

eMail Address:_____

Credit Card: ❑ Visa   ❑ Master Card ❑ AMEX

Credit Card#:_____

Expiration Date:_____

Billing Address:_____

_____

City:_____

State/ZIP:_____

Country:_____

PRICE: $29.95 ($US) plus $5.00 ($US) S&H ... *Per Book!*

CA Residents Add 8.25% Sales Tax
International Orders Add $5.00 ($US) EXTRA Per Book

TOTAL $ _____ ENCLOSED!

Prices and availability subject to change without notice. Please allow one to three weeks for delivery. Thank you for your order!